This book was published as part of the exhibition
Home Made - Create, Produce, Live
presented by the CID - centre for innovation and design at Grand-Hornu (Belgium) from
15 October 2023 to 11 February 2024

HOME MADE

CREATE · PRODUCE · LIVE

Curated by Fabien Petiot and Chloé Braunstein-Kriegel

TABLE OF CONTENTS

FOREWORD — 7
Marie Pok

INTRODUCTION — 9
Fabien Petiot and Chloé Braunstein-Kriegel

WORKING REMOTELY, FROM HOME, THEN AND NOW — 17
Didier Terrier

DESIGN FOR HOME-BASED WORK. FROM ARCHITECTURAL HISTORY TO CONTEMPORARY INNOVATION — 31
Frances Holliss

1 THE HOME WORKSHOP: THE INTERMINGLING OF WORK AND PERSONAL LIFE

Introduction — 43
Fabien Petiot and Chloé Braunstein-Kriegel

The chambrelans of Limoges — 45
Ariane Aujoulat

Home factories: The photographic investigation of Antony Neuckens around 1910 — 48
Fabien Petiot and Chloé Braunstein-Kriegel

New technologies in the home: a post-industrial "relocation"? — 52
Fabien Petiot and Chloé Braunstein-Kriegel

Exhibited works — 54

2 WORKING IN THE HOME

Introduction — 63
Fabien Petiot and Chloé Braunstein-Kriegel

Repairability: technological skills of ordinary people — 67
Fabien Petiot and Chloé Braunstein-Kriegel

House Music, the origins of a domestic sound — 70
Christophe Vix-Gras

Hair, a highly sentimental raw material — 73
Antonin Mongin

Exhibited works — 76

3 THE CONFINED TIME OF DOMESTIC SPACE

Introduction   81
Fabien Petiot and Chloé Braunstein-Kriegel

The "bricoleur", in a kind of perpetual lockdown   84
Fabien Petiot and Chloé Braunstein-Kriegel

The new Robinson Crusoes   89
Fabien Petiot and Chloé Braunstein-Kriegel

Exhibited works   92

4 THE BUILDING, A "MACHINE FOR LIVING IN"

Introduction   99
Fabien Petiot and Chloé Braunstein-Kriegel

**The "model apartment", or the emergence
of new domestic landscapes**   101
Fabien Petiot and Chloé Braunstein-Kriegel

Architectural modularity: the *à la carte* home   104
Fabien Petiot and Chloé Braunstein-Kriegel

Collective housing, an augmented habitat?   107
Fabien Petiot and Chloé Braunstein-Kriegel

Exhibited works   110

WHEN WORKING FROM HOME SHAPES THE CITY AND THE LANDSCAPE   **118**
Fabien Petiot and Chloé Braunstein-Kriegel

BIBLIOGRAPHY   **130**

CREDITS   **139**

FOREWORD

In the late 1970s, in my own family in Singapore, women experienced semi-industrial work at home on a daily basis. The small family business made electrical cables. Plugs were used to connect lamps or household appliances were connected to, which the company sold to various customers, including Philips. My uncles would bring home endless lengths of cable. My aunts and the less unruly children among us had the task of cutting them into sections of equal length. You had to be precise and line up your piece of cable up with the yardstick: the coffee table. Every evening, after dinner, we would cut up these cables while eating rambutans and grumbling. Work that was not declared, not paid and not safe... Family work. The next day it would all go off to the factory. Some pieces would still be a little sticky from the juice of the fruit we had eaten while working.

Production norms and standards have come a long way since then. So has working from home. Once banned, then brought back into favour by the possibilities introduced of remote working, it is now in the spotlight, and raising all sorts of questions. Behind this personal, anecdotal experience, that which was lost when the coffee table was once again used for fruit bowls and tea sets, is that strange connection between workers within the same family, whether they wanted to work or not, sharing the same tools and intimate space. When the lockdown sent workers, children and students home, they had to find that same connection, or at least a way of living, a way of sharing our indoor spaces, our working tools, our daily tasks. Returning to work at home raises many more questions than those relating to organisation or output. It also challenges our social connections, our family relationships, the way we live and work together. The way we respond is not always positive. Such circumstances can lead to violence and exploitation. But they also offer an unmissable opportunity to rethink our chains and scales of production, our standards and yardsticks (a Chinese coffee table does the job very well), our mobility, our family relationships or how we live together, do business together or create together...

Torn between consumerist productivism and new climate and social challenges, design finds its way, through trial and error, just as we might try out a new recipe at home. Making or repairing things yourself is another immense source of satisfaction and joy that we would like to remind people of, especially through the creative workshops that the CID - center for innovation and design organises alongside its exhibitions. With the Home Made exhibition, the CID continues to sound out the world, to listen to these new experiences that help us move forward... and sometimes take us back to our roots.

MARIE POK,
Director of the CID - center for innovation and design at Grand-Hornu

Fig. 1: Martial Marquet, *Bureau idéal*, 2020
Recycled wood, plant fibres, recycled foam, plaster and acrylic resin

INTRODUCTION

Fabien Petiot and Chloé Braunstein-Kriegel

Fascinated by production methods and how they fit in with the challenges of a particular period, while witnessing the spread of remote working, it has dawned on us, ironically, that we, as exhibition curators and designers, have ourselves never ceased to be home workers, whether full time or only occasionally. Is it because the reality of a long shared experience has finally been put into words? Or is it that this way of working at home suddenly became more visible and legitimate, having been the norm for a long time, before it lost its credibility? Whatever the reason, these thoughts led us to look at the question "What do I make at home?" repeated endlessly during the 2020-21 COVID-19 lockdowns. The complete overhaul of our relationship with work has turned the very notion of "at home" upside down. We feel that these questions, which are both straightforward and complex – what does living mean? what does working mean? – deserve to be discussed in the same place. It seems like a good idea for us to join the dots intuitively, generously, but also scientifically, through speaking to researchers who have long been interested in a return to working from home.

At a time when remote working has become mainstream in our minds, when technology is making it easier to establish a growing number of professional tasks at home, what links are being forged between work and life? Between inside and outside spaces? With working from home, the world enters the house, the house becomes the world: your habitat is connected to the city and innervates it, blurring the traditional boundaries between public and private. To attempt to respond to the complexity of this new landscape, and for an easier understanding, we have defined four different spaces – WORKSHOP, HOME, RESIDENTIAL BUILDING, and lastly, NEIGH-BOURHOOD, CITY, and even stretching it to REGION. Thanks to the exhibition *Home Made – Create, Produce, Live* and this accompanying publication, these four spaces have helped us to think about the rich history of working from home, with the forward thinking and creativity of contemporary designers and architects, makers and craftspeople. The living environment, an inspirational place if ever there was one, is presented here as a space in which you can produce and express yourself, the epicentre of reflection on what we "make" at home, both literally and figuratively, whether as amateurs or professionals. Everything leads us to believe that the future is being made from home, an exciting place that brings together the personal, the political, the economic, the cultural and the social, all under one roof.

Craftsmanship and its artefacts, topics on everybody's lips (until recently), will have been much more than a fad at a time when we are all desperately seeking meaning.[1] In reality, we are witnessing the normalisation of our revised relationship with "doing". The Covid-19 crisis, a moment of acceleration and hypertrophy of earlier phenomena, served as a reminder of its presence in everyday life and, by the same token, of its legitimacy in the domestic sphere. It is against this backdrop that we witnessed the production of masks and respirators by makers at the height of the 2020 crisis, alongside the celebration of manual activities and repairs. We should also remember the significant increase in the purchase of household appliances, many of which were worthy of professional use, during the lockdowns, or the growth of tutorials dedicated to manual jobs. Simultaneously and complementarily, the omnipresence of digital technology, the proliferation of electronic services and the networking of skills have helped to speed up this movement.

Creative individuals, whether architects, artists, designers or makers, translate ideas, innovations and changing aspirations into ways of life. The *Home Made* exhibition focuses on their anticipation of the spread of the notion of working in private spaces and its impact on a wider landscape. These creatives are, after all, inhabitants like everyone else! But the way in which they now dream means to appropriate the domestic sphere and embrace its characteristic themes reveals how their work has evolved. A few decades ago, it seemed inconceivable for most designers and architects to work anywhere other than in an office or a space dedicated to work, whether they were employees or *freelancers*. Nor was there any question of making things by yourself, in other words at home. This was the preserve of craftspeople, with whom industrial designers did not fully identify.

The super powers of the home
The introduction of tools facilitating artisanal or industrial production is one of the themes covered by the *Home Made* exhibition. Skills are acquired by practically applying them (*learning by doing*), from your own home, with the resources you have to hand. These capabilities are also nurtured by knowledge shared within interest-based communities, whether amateur or professional. This covers a broad spectrum of activities, from producing your own objects using digital tools (3D printing, laser cutter etc.) to more intuitive experiences: drawing or improvisation, or even "robinsonade". The levels of action encompass both architectural rehabilitation and electronic repairs, for example. The complexity may vary, from making your own crockery to building machines designed for your specific needs or project. A loom producing large volumes of fabric, the creation of a workshop-scale foundry to produce all the hardware that a building site needs, or a home studio where you can come up with your own musical compositions: these activities remind us of the principle of "self-production" developed by philosopher Ivan Illich.[2]

---

1 Petiot and Braunstein-Kriegel 2018.

2 Illich 2021.

For him, it was about satisfying your own needs using resources and technical means available locally. This re-appropriation of production tools encourages individual autonomy and savoir-faire, thus contributing to a more sustainable society.

Through the projects on display in the exhibition, we can imagine their creators are striving for a form of self-sufficiency that lives alongside a keen environmental awareness: they are interested in manifest, often experimental, ways of producing ushered into the home. Working at home can ultimately change our living environments, in the same way that our neighbourhoods and our towns, and even the countryside, are affected by the growth in this kind of activities. Digital technology contributes to these forward-thinking visions, where the home is bestowed with an incredible power: its inhabitants can have an impact on the world from the comfort of their own homes.

To support these thoughts about the role played by the domestic space today, we felt it was essential that we draw on a specific period in the history of working from home, namely the proto-industrial age in Europe of the early 19th to the first half of the 20th centuries. This period witnessed production methods that were halfway between craftsmanship and industry, demonstrating the pervasive power of work, which became visible in interiors, architecture and urban planning. However, now as in the past, working from home forces us to ask the question about how gender roles affect the way environments, from private spaces to cities themselves, are organised. So, when in 1910, Belgian Antony Neuckens carried out his famous photographic study of home workshops, it blatantly revealed the urgent need to do something about the appalling insalubrious living conditions of impoverished workers (Fig. 6, 10, 20). But the solutions put forward in terms of urban planning did not take socialisation into account when establishing their priorities, and so as a result, certain categories of individuals, and particularly women who mainly worked from home, became invisible. These neighbourhoods that were either redesigned or built from scratch in the middle of the 20th century, then to promote post-war reconstruction after 1945, were once bustling, industrious, vibrant areas. They were now gradually emptied of any activity, resulting in the isolation of working-class women, relegated to their domestic place. Although dismissed from the employment market according to prevailing conservative ideology,[3] they were in no way released from labour, but rather assigned to "*shadow work*".[4] Nevertheless, in recent decades, the growing presence of women in the world of work, the spread of digital tools, and now the geographical dispersion associated with how the service industries are organised to allow remote working, mean that it would be worth decision-makers considering an overhaul of this now out-dated urban model. Against this backdrop, working from home could

---

3 Holliss 2015, p. 130. She refers back to the arguments put forward by Jane Jacobs in *The Death and Life of Great American Cities* (1961), a pamphlet against America's urban planners and property developers in the 1950-60s.

4 Illich 1981.

enjoy a prime position, as architectural historian Frances Holliss recommends. She campaigns for more recognition of this form of activity, which is an integral part of how towns and cities should be considered today.

These ideas, in keeping with the resolutely forward-thinking approach of our work, are backed by the principle of the "15-minute city" and the model of "Doughnut Cities". They pave the way for social and environmental sustainability, which cities like Amsterdam, Berlin and Melbourne have already begun to embrace. Here, more generally, it is about the conditions for urban resilience that turn the ability to adapt to all sorts of difficulties (health crises, environment and environmental issues etc.) into a major positive advantage. These models fully incorporate working from home into their implementation.

The city, our other home

Moving in centrifugal motions, "from the spoon to the city",[5] is not just inspiring, it's also a founding principle of an all-encompassing vision of design. Theorists and designers of modernity have also built their approach on this mutual influence of scales of magnitude. Following the example of the series of works published in the 1840s onwards, in which the American theorist and educator Catharine Beecher offered advice to women on how to arrange their homes

and in particular the kitchen, transposing the model of the industrial production chain to the domestic world. Of course, this approach has to be considered within some context. In slave-owning America in the first half of the 19th century, Beecher wanted to demonstrate an approach to design which, by allowing people to do without slaves, could contribute to the Abolitionist cause. She also wanted to promote the emancipation of women[6] by streamlining the tasks assigned to them. For his part, William Morris drew on the conditions in which objects were produced in the Victoria era to build a social utopia, campaign to protect nature, and achieve nothing less than happiness. Today, in line with these great reformers, how can remote working, and more generally production and creativity at home, contribute to a new model?

The notion of "ville à domicile"[7] helps us figure out this cause and effect chain, from the privacy of the home to globalisation. It refers to activities which usually take place in towns and cities, but are now happening in the home as well. Working, studying, self-care, shopping, admin, educating oneself, exercising or socialising: these have all become commonplace activities in living rooms and bedrooms. The exponential growth of online shopping and meal deliveries at any time of the day contributes to this retreat into the home, synonymous with

---

5 "Dal cucchiaio alla città" ("From the spoon to the city") was the slogan of Italian architect and theorist Ernesto Nathan Rogers in the 1950s, probably inspired by Hermann Muthesius and his "Vom Sofakissen zum Stadtebau" (From sofa cushions to city-buildings) which, in 1911, was used as the plan for the Deutscher Werkbund.

6 In particular, she wrote with her sister, Harriet Beecher Stowe, author of *Uncle Tom's Cabin* (1852). See Beecher 2008; Beecher 2009; Midal 2009, pp. 23-26; Clarisse 2004.

7 Literally, "city at home", an expression invented by the Agence d'urbanisme et d'aménagement de Toulouse aire métropolitaine (AUAT) following studies carried out in 2021-2022 in order to help communities and stakeholders embrace ongoing urban, social, economic and environmental developments.

comfort. But all of this is also based on profound logistical and social change. The viability of transport costs and services depends on reliance on a precarious workforce, one of the features of the now omnipresent *uberisation*. It is based on a new infrastructure that is seeing the proliferation of small storage spaces altering the urban landscape (think about the *dark store* phenomenon), perhaps heralding the decline of the large shopping areas on the outskirts of towns and along major roads. In other words, getting a new computer cable or some shopping a few hours after placing your order ultimately affects whole regions. So talking about working from home means asking questions about contemporary habitability and also trying to understand, when it comes to the home, what the landscape will look like in the future.

A Time of one's own

Saving time plays a crucial role in this reconstruction of our environment, while paradoxically, the number of hours we spend working keeps on increasing. All sorts of smartphone apps help us navigate the new working landscape, outside the four walls of the office. Towns and cities have become an extension of the home and now provide the backdrop for our work: cafés, co-working spaces and hotel lounges are becoming

Fig. 2: Marie Jacotey, *Granby Four Streets*, drawing, 2015

alternative locations for nomadic workers in their own right, while the *mobility hubs*[8] model is taking shape. This permanent capacity to adapt, demonstrated both by workers and by the spaces in which they inhabit, is contagious: for example, it reflects the reversibility and modularity of buildings, an idea that is by no means new, but that makes more sense now than ever before. Once again, it's an all-encompassing vision that is taking shape. The spread of remote working is thus presented as a way of resolving the inefficient use of space when residential neighbourhoods are deserted during working hours, and business districts are abandoned overnight and at the weekend.[9]

The creative talents brought together within the *Home Made* exhibition are nurturing another relationship with time. They include trial-and-error textile experiments in Hella Jongerius's workshop (Fig. 58, the slow spinning of silkworms used by Iris Seuren to create a piece of clothing (Fig. 31), or the time it would take to grow latex-rich plants in the scenario imagined by Marco Federico Cagnoni (Fig. 73, 74). The process of gathering materials leads to the creation of the object over different time frames (Emma Cogné's PVC tubes (Fig. 77, 78), the aluminium used by Ciguë) (Fig. 75, 76), the wooden branches assembled by Erwan Bouroullec (Fig. 50, 56) from the long, sluggish amount of time required for research to the urgency of improvisation. It's also about the pleasure of making

and creating, alone or together, for example by learning repair techniques. Doing things yourself, alone or together, mobilises a level of attention - or should we say affection - reminiscent of the DIY enthusiast. Making things, alone or with others, mobilises a level of attention - or should we say affection - reminiscent of the do-it-yourself enthusiast, the aptly named "bricoleur"[10] in French. The commitment is total, from Stéphane Bureaux's production of casein protein bowls (Fig. 48), a cross between a recipe and a lab experiment, to the Basket-club collective's playful and innovative wickerwork (Fig. 53, 61-67). In the end, it's about reconciling the long life of buildings with our ever-changing lives, by offering a modular architecture that users can make their own, as in the case of the projects carried out by the Wald agency (Fig. 3, 68, 71-72).

All of these designers and architects are keenly aware of the need to make most of their time. They also have a proven taste for the workshop and the intimacy of their production. In fact, for these creators, there is a need to maintain what Virginia Woolf referred to as *A room of one's own*.[11] But just as literature is inconceivable without a reader, what we make at home is not a selfish pleasure. It is a mirror that we hold up to our time: will what is produced (intellectually and physically) in the future be touched by a certain individualism that will drive us to make things solely for ourselves? Or will

---

8   Frame Lab 2022, p. 129. Bus stops and station forecourts can be transformed into temporary working spaces associated with businesses and services, charging points for electric vehicles, parcel collection lockers and bicycle garages.

9   Holliss 2015, p. 170.

10 Jarreau 1985.

11 Woolf 2020. In 1929, Virginia Woolf was analysing the difficult living conditions of women writers who were deprived of their own dedicated space.

we all come together, with everyone contributing to a network or a community? Against this backdrop, where living and making spaces are inextricably linked, stakeholders in towns and cities should begin thinking now about an environment that responds to the emergence of a rich web of creators, small-scale producers, home workers and users who are invested in their living environment.

Fig. 3: Wald, *Proto-Habitat*, installation in a public garden in Bordeaux, France, 2020

Fig. 4: V. Spahn (illustration), *Celles qu'on oublie. Les ouvrières à domicile (The forgotten ones. Women working at home)*, 1914, booklet for the song by Xavier Privas, Henri Gaillard Publisher, BNF, Paris, France (inv. FRBNF43216850)

WORKING REMOTELY, FROM HOME, THEN AND NOW

Didier Terrier,
Professor emeritus at the Université Polytechnique des Hauts-de-France, specialising in the history of labour in the 18th and 19th centuries

One of the most dramatic effects of the 2020 pandemic was that a proportion of people's working activities moved from the office to people's homes in order to reconcile the need for a lockdown for health reasons with the need for work to carry on. In France, for example, the proportion of employees who worked remotely at the height of the health crisis between March 2020 and February 2021 was somewhere between 15% and 25%. Designed to combat the spread of the virus, remote working was not a new idea however: a significant minority of workers had already been working remotely to some extent, throughout Western Europe, for two or even three decades. However, encouraged by the health authorities, practised en masse by *front office*[1] workers, and facilitated by the widespread use of digital solutions, its legitimacy rose. While it had struggled to become established, in a matter of weeks, working remotely became a norm, and then a habit. Some saw in this, quite naturally, a foreshadowing of what could be, in the near future, a key component in a new way of organising the space in which work is done, with remote working playing a key role.[2] In contrast, few observed a resurgence of age-old practices in this revival of working from home. However, in order to bring together worlds of work that until this point had been so alien to each other for such a long time, it was important to avoid falling into some anachronistic traps.[3]

Rediscovering the long term in the light of the present

To mark the return of home working to the mainstream of how working practices are organised, Deloitte's announcement that it would reduce its office space in the City of London in April 2022, at a time when the pandemic was abating, was symbolic. Hindered by technical and technological shortcomings, remote work had got off to a relatively slow start two or three decades earlier. Although it seemed to have a promising future, it felt as though it would take a very long time to implement changes in terms of how work was organised and where it would take place. However, the auditing and consultancy giant was betting on having more employees than individu-

---

1 The *front office* encompasses everyone who, by the nature of their work, is allowed to work remotely, at least partially, as opposed to those in the *back office*, i.e. essential workers who must be present at their workplace at all times.

2 Remote working began in the 1960s but it did not become commonplace for a long time. See *Future Shock* (Toffler 1972) in which Alvin Toffler nevertheless included it as one of the features that foresaw in post-industrial society. The book sold over 6 million copies and was a huge success.

3 Vernant 2004.

al offices available by making remote working more common, sometimes on a full-time and sometimes on a part-time basis. In doing so, it was handing back a third of its premises to the property market, with the intention of making substantial savings, given the rental prices in the heart of the British capital. Deloitte also seemed to be keeping some of its staff happy, including those keen to reduce the length and frequency of their journeys within such a huge city. By doing this, it was dramatically and symbolically creating a framework for a return to a more disparate way of organising work that had prevailed in many previous centuries.[4]

Because, at the other end of a chronological period spanning five or six centuries, two ways of organising work at home prevailed in turn, when they didn't overlap, as the 18th century became the 19th century. The first, which had its roots in the 15th century, was what the Germans call the *Kaufsystem*: peasant-workers supplied themselves with raw materials and independently managed the sale of their products, which were usually produced during the farming off-season. The second, in the 17th century, was the *Verlagssystem*, which began to spread and really flourished when raw materials – such as fine merino wool or cotton – had to be imported to make products to meet the needs of the changing market. This required financial resources that people did not have in the countryside,

and justified the involvement of trader-manufacturers from the city who, in addition to becoming part of the commercial channels, began to take control of the work that had become geographically dispersed. This system completely transformed the relationship between those involved, because this time, work was organised in a much more interventionist way: the use of the raw materials handed over by the trader-manufacturers to the peasant-workers was now supervised to a greater or lesser extent to prevent the misappropriation of materials or product defects. This is why foremen came to regulate this new way of distributing work with varying degrees of strictness.

But what does the remote working that many professionals do today have in common with the abundance of energy of the lace maker at her pillow[5] or the weaver hunched over his loom all day? Separated by over three centuries, is the fact that they both work at home enough to see a similarity between such dissimilar situations? And yet they all see their work taking place in spaces that, whether locally or globally, no longer have any limits.[6] This is obviously the case today where, in many ways, distances disappear in the era of globalisation, the Internet and *globish*. But this was also the case in previous centuries: the lace maker and the weaver were established, sometimes without their knowledge, in a world economy responding to the pace

---

4 Thomas 2022.

5 The pillow is the cushion used to make lace, with the help of bobbins.

6 This is why they are distinguished from craftsmen and tradesmen whose activity is essentially on a much smaller scale.

of international markets, far removed from local or regional economic environments. Lastly, they are all caught up in a network of hierarchical relationships that cut through the walls of personal space, so that professional tensions are invited into a home that ceases to be a refuge. As a result, in all situations and at all times, personal space is subject to a process of alienation which, however it is experienced, blurs the boundaries between the different time frames of existence.

Home-based work and the rise of capitalism

While the spread of home-based industry in the countryside had been known about for a long time, it was during the 1970s and 1980s that the American historian Franklin Mendels[7] constructed a general system to explain the transition from agrarian societies to the industrial world in the late 18th- early 19th century, based on multiple activities going on in villages. As this was based on the ability of the big traders in manufacturing towns and cities to play on the versatility of peasant-workers to supply the large trading networks with sometimes expensive products, Mendels felt this represented more or less finely honed forms of a model that he described as proto-industrialisation.[8] No historian before him had foreseen the link that existed between the move of so many

Fig. 5: *Women's meeting ("couvige" - meeting of lace makers) in the heart of the village,* date unknown, Puy-de-Dôme departmental archives, France (inv. no. 569 Fi 1061)

7 Franklin Mendels (1943-1988), an expert in economic history, known among other things for the concept of proto-industrialisation.
8 Mendels 198.

activities related to working the land to the home and the biological balance of the populations concerned. When the labour market opened up, it became materially possible to start a family earlier. Drawing on a field study in Flemish rural areas in the 18th century, he concluded that the resulting lowering of the marriageable age led to an increase in fertility, even in poor and overpopulated areas. We witnessed the establishment of a kind of "reserve army", essential when it came to ultimately feeding the rural exodus, the growth of towns and cities and the formation of industrial populations. In addition, the trader-manufacturers, thanks to their accumulation of wealth, also played an important role in the early accumulation of capital: this was an essential prerequisite for financing the concentration and mechanisation of manufacturing production. According to Mendels, proto-industrialisation thus contributed decisively to the transition from the *domestic system* established in the 15th century to the factory system, which spread at different rates and in different ways from one region to another, and from one product to another.

Fig. 6: Antony Neuckens, *Production of staple bags*, circa 1910, photograph on glass plate, (éd. Soullier) Mundaneum, Mons, Belgium

By stimulating research, this model led to undeniable advances in the understanding of pre-industrial economies and societies on the one hand, and the transition to the industrial world itself on the other.[9] But the role of home-based industries did not end there. Between the 1780s and the 1830s, a second proto-industrial age took root, which could be regarded as having lasted until the 1950s. With the rise of mechanisation and the proliferation of factories, in towns and cities as well as in the countryside, it managed to compensate for the technical inadequacies of machines, thus ensuring the production of the most delicate objects. It also guaranteed flexibility of production at particularly busy times, without the need to acquire new equipment, all the while keeping workers, who were often in the process of becoming proletarianised, in the countryside. In this way, in the eyes of the 19th century bigwigs, this was a good way of limiting the accumulation of working but dangerous classes in the towns and cities.[10] As the second proto-industrial age spread to the towns and cities, it finally succeeded in satisfying alternative types of production that were based on widespread, light industries, made up of a range of different approaches to production or manual activities.

Other forms of home-based work, this time mainly based in urban areas, began to flourish in the mid-19th century. Some workers had no choice but to agree to the *sweating system*:[11] tucked away in attics or cubbyholes, usually out of sight, they had to "sweat", in other words work long hours to earn a living. In the textile industry, for example, where the cost of subcontracted work was extremely low, workers made objects and clothes by hand, as well as making accessories such as artificial flowers or mending clothes, demanding a huge amount of punishing extra work. This form of home-based work was intended to be a move towards niche markets, as an alternative to the mass production of the factory system.[12] Large traders could thus be very responsive to the ever-changing nature of the markets. The invention of "confection" (literally "finished" clothing, so mass-produced by definition) available in "boutiques de nouveautés" (novelty shops) in the 1830s and then in department stores from the Second Empire onwards, and then the invention of "prêt-à-porter", or ready-to-wear, clothing in the 1950s, did a great deal to drive advances in this area. By the 1880s, the electric motor revolution had given a new impetus to home-based work, particularly through the widespread use of the sewing machine. This reinvention of dispersed industry became so important that in France in 1936, one third of working women were still working at home.[13] Then, with strong

---

9 Coll. 1981.

10 Chevalier 1958 and Kalifa 2013.

11 This term refers to the exploitation of workers by their employers through excessive working hours, low wages, insalubrious working conditions etc. It was mainly used during the first industrial revolution. See Barraud 2014.

12 Green 1998.

13 Avrane 2013.

competition from products from countries where labour was much cheaper, this method of production withered and finally disappeared in the 1980s.

Today, the resurgence of remote working is too recent to measure all of its implications for the history of capitalism. It seems clear, however, that there is a risk that it will transform social relations in businesses, encouraging more individualisation among workers. As long as employees are rarely working remotely for more than two days a week, the link with colleagues and the hierarchy is not broken. Beyond that, the world of work may be completely turned upside down, in which case we could be experiencing the early days of the biggest change to work since the progressive establishment of the division of labour and then of assembly line work.[14]

Geographical logistics of the spread of home working

At the moment, its great capacity for fluidity means that remote working can fit into all the possible configurations of a given network, as technology allows everyone, or almost everyone, to connect and produce, for the most part, intangible goods from any location, as long as there is... connection. It is true that Internet coverage is still a source of inequality between different regions, to the extent that it sometimes impedes the urban exodus dreamt about by city dwellers in search of a different quality of life from the one offered by an urban environment. But conversely, in a country the size of France, for example, a large number of pleasant countryside areas, sunny coastlines or, even more so, medium-sized towns (*zoom towns* like Angers or Avignon, for example) are now welcoming workers who have chosen to work from home in an attractive setting rather than commute every day between soulless suburbs and charmless office buildings in the middle of a big city. It is worth remembering that in Western European countries today, between a quarter and a third of jobs are compatible with remote working. In some European capitals, such as Paris, it is more like half, although this proportion rises to three quarters when it comes to managers and senior professionals (this is also a way of implying the limits of the spread of home working, which is not necessarily for the lowlier ranks who are, paradoxically, the "essential" workers).

This relative flexibility in the spatial distribution of home-based work today contrasts with the much more restrictive geographical logistics that there used to be. The production of semi-finished or finished goods required less expansion of the productive territory in order to limit the extent of the distribution and collection channels for semi-finished or finished products. In addition, there was a need for hydroelectric power or the proximity of a transport network, and for a large, docile, inexpensive and skilled workforce. This is why the dissemination of villages that were "hives of industries", within easy reach of the city's rich traders, was usually the result of a deliberate

---

14 Leroi and Mettetal 2023.

effort to organise the territory. In northern France, for example, Saint-Quentin and Valenciennes were at the centre of a nebulous group of rural weavers, all of whom produced fine linen cloth for the major international markets.[15] There were similar set-ups in towns and cities. As early as the 18th century, "chambrelans" (literally somebody who worked in a "chambre", or room), would accumulate within invisible borders, identifying a particular street, a block of flats, a building, a neighbourhood for their labours. In Paris, the Saint-Antoine district was famous for this. Here, solidarity, apprenticeships and competition were the main criteria, especially when a space enjoyed a strong identity around a particularly typical product. The Croix-Rousse district in Lyon in the 19th century thus came to symbolise silk work, and the architecture of the façades of the houses where the "canuts", or silk-weavers, lived bore witness to an easily identifiable activity.[16] Obviously this is no longer the case. Working at home, seen from the street, is hidden. Only the regular presence of remote workers in their homes is evidence to the neighbourhood that they use digital tools to carry out their work at home.

Fig. 7: Antony Neuckens, *Intérieur d'un coupeur gantier (A glove maker's home workshop)*, circa 1910, photograph on glass plate, Mundaneum, Mons, Belgium (inv. ARC-MUND-PV-TD-027

15 Terrier 1998 (A).
16 Saunier 1992.

Work invades the private sphere

How, then, can we now find a sustainable way to characterise the private space in which remote work has become permanently embedded? Technical requirements become a prerequisite for the way the entire domestic space is organised. Setting up the loom in the cellar of the cloth maker was thus an absolute necessity: the atmosphere required for yarn not to break had to ensure the right humidity, and the lighting required architectural adaptations that signalled the presence of a proto-industrial family to the road or alley outside thanks to the introduction of large windows.[17] Today, in some cases, the office, with its computer equipment, ergonomic chair and shelves of folders, also indicates the existence of a working room in the home. Family life is theoretically excluded, as this is a specialist, separate room.

But in contrast, some activities, especially when they are temporary or intermittent, do not require any special arrangements and can be taken from one room to another. The material features of the space becomes less about an area adapted to specific tasks than about connectivity. Of course, in previous centuries, other ways of working could lead to the existence of nomadic locations at multiple sites. The weaver only had to move her spinning wheel, the basket maker his wicker, and the pin-maker his tools. Many other "light" instruments and tools did not require a specific space and thus contributed to blurring the boundaries between work and home life, especially when, in towns and cities especially, the whole family lived in a single room.[18]

It is interesting to look at the few engravings and photographs of home-based work available from the late 19th century. What prevails then is, if not disorder, at least a mixing up of the equipment essential for work and things to do with family life, leisure, etc. In this sense, the confusion of spatial norms goes back to that of temporal norms: carrying out two activities at the same time, one professional, the other domestic, can be understood today in the same way: the presence of a hot plate or a cradle is combined with that of a laptop, a smartphone, a tablet etc. For that matter, look at the extent to which each individual's place in the home is gendered when the work at home involves all or some of the adults in the family. Because from the remote working of today to the proto-industrial activities of the past, it is usually the men who appropriate the space for themselves and relegate mothers, wives and daughters to situations where it is much easier to blur the lines between domestic tasks and professional life. It is true that there are no clear-cut rules in the gendered division of labour, and in the economy of the Alps, for example, women did very well for themselves: when seasonal migration took their husbands away from home for long periods of time, they wore the trousers at home. But these were, of course, exceptions.

---

17 Terrier 1998 (B).

18 Roche 1981.

In Italy, in the Valtellina, leather work and silk weaving drove men to carry out the rewarding, remunerative tasks, while the women took on the ancillary obligations and other subordinate tasks connected to working the land, among other things.[19] Nowadays, women who work at home find it no easier to reconcile work and personal or family life.[20] To such an extent that they are blamed when they can't manage it all, unlike men, for whom working at home is much more easily accompanied by an exemption from the mental burden of everything that is not part of their job itself. The few testimonies we have on the way in which each individual occupied the domestic space to work in the past say the same thing: working at home never had the same implications for the different genders, except in the social relationships with those placing the orders for products.[21]

Working at home, professional solidarity and competition

It remains to be seen how we will look back at the professional and social relationships between those who spend most of their time at home and are connected to each other only by often invisible threads. Sometimes the collective protest of workers based in different places emerges during the course of history. The exasperation of

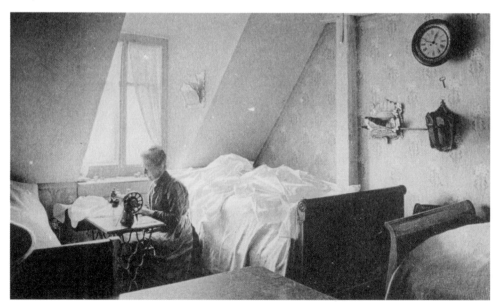

Fig. 8: Antony Neuckens, *Lingère (Linen maker)*, circa 1910, photograph on glass plate, Mundaneum, Mons, Belgium (inv. ARC-MUND-DIAV-TD-016_72

19 Lorenzetti 2012.
20 This is clearly the case in the Swiss and Italian valleys of Valais (Switzerland) and Valtellina (Italy) in the late 19th and early 20th centuries. Lorenzetti 2012 Ibid.
21 Terrier 2021, pp. 23.

English peasant-workers confronted with declining living conditions in the early 19th century, the uprising of the "canuts"[22] in Lyon under the July Monarchy in France, the Silesian weavers' uprising in June 1844: they may be well-known, but these movements are exceptions, because dispersion tends to dilute rather than crystallise tensions and recriminations against the people in charge. While the spread of working from home is now less often associated than it used to be with a high degree of isolation, less social protection and poor pay, the balance of power remains unbalanced between disparate workers on the one hand, and employers on the other. Even if space-time has been abolished today thanks to technology, the disappearance or rarefaction of daily relationships reduces the potential forms of solidarity between workers who have become scattered in this way. Indeed, many employers see "working from home" as a good way of encouraging healthy competition between their employees. Some of them are not ruling out the idea of paving the

Fig. 9: Antony Neuckens (attributed to), *Dentellière de Bruges (Bruges lace maker)*, circa 1910, photograph on glass plate, Mundaneum, Mons, Belgium (inv. ARC-MUNDA-PVD-000002_72)

---

22 The Canut Revolts refers to a number of uprisings by silk-weavers that took place in Lyon, France, in 1831, 1834 and 1848.

way for what could be, in the near future, a new trigger for relocating work outside of Europe.[23] In short, when industrial relations are tense, the dispersion of employees never bodes well, especially when there is conflict to be resolved in their favour.

At first glance, working at home sounds appealing, as it seems to offer more choice about how time is spent. But while it's easy to see the benefits of working remotely, its disadvantages come to light more slowly: employees are alone when they have to tackle what work needs to be done, the pace of the daily or weekly working times to be imposed, the level of remuneration to be negotiated, and job security to be consolidated. In short, in this regard, working remotely is both alienating and emancipating. Under these conditions, working at home is never, by definition, a panacea for having full control over one's professional activity, free from the constraints imposed by the hierarchy of social relations of production. If we look to the past, Lyon's big silk merchants, worried about the aggression of the canuts, embraced practices used in the 18th century in the second third of the 19th century and distributed work throughout the countryside around Lyon, justifiably convinced that the peasant-workers dispersed throughout rural areas would be more docile, accept lower wages and work longer hours.[24]

In short, in the past as in the present, working from home has an impact on rhythms of work: if each individual can, in this way, cultivate the feeling of choosing his or her constraints, the interweaving of working hours with other social activities risks blurring the boundaries between different time frames, to the point of allowing professional tasks to invade daily life. Because, paradoxically, rather than giving you a sense of freedom, taking control of your own time can in fact impose a level of dependency: when you are imposing it on yourself, your working timetable can put your free will to the test. Even if the contingencies of everyday life provide good reasons to move on, you need to know how to avoid harbouring feelings of guilt. Because more often than not, working at home is like walking a tightrope where there is a constant risk of losing "time to recharge your batteries, to refocus on yourself, to let your mind wander, all of which are vital ways to shore up an efficient, calm approach to work".[25] Indeed, the tyranny of your own high standards can sometimes be even worse than those imposed from the outside, so much so that it can become a poisoned chalice.

---

23 The vulnerability of those working from home forced to compete with one another by their bosses is discussed in an ILO report, "Working from home: From invisibility to decent work", dated 13 January 2021.

24 Cayez 1981.

25 Barth 2022.

Fig. 10: Antony Neuckens, *Tailleurs (Tailors)*, c. 1910, photograph on glass plate, Mundaneum, Mons, Belgium (inv. ARC-MUND-PV-TD-032

Fig. 11: Weavers "topshops", 1857, Kingfield, Coventry, United Kingdom

DESIGN FOR HOME-BASED WORK. FROM ARCHITECTURAL HISTORY TO CONTEMPORARY INNOVATION

Frances Holliss
Architect and Emeritus Reader of Architecture at London Metropolitan University. Founder and Director of the *Workhome Project*.

Home. Pre-Covid, there was a widely accepted understanding of home as a place to cook, eat, bathe, sleep, watch TV and bring up children. For more than a century, housing has been designed around the limited domestic needs of the nuclear family - and the broad-brush formula of kitchen/dining/living rooms/bedrooms/bathrooms, with a garden or balcony for the lucky. Houses and apartments have also, increasingly, been conceived as standard products in an international investment market, designed tight-fit to minimal space standards to maximise profit. Its central role to provide space for people's lives somewhat diminished as a result, the housing stock has failed to reflect significant changes to household and lifestyle - including the steady increase, over the past 20 years, in the number of people working from home.[1] While based on the findings of research carried out largely in the UK 2003-2023,[2] these observations can undoubtedly be extended to Europe - and to Western countries more generally.

The pandemic has provided a wake-up call. As it swept across the world, and social distancing was necessary to reduce the spread of the virus, many governments strongly encouraged or mandated working from home.[3] By April 2020, almost half of the UK working population was working from home[4] and by the second quarter of 2020, the global home-based workforce had reached an estimated 557m.[5] This meant homes that had not been conceived or designed as such were in use as workplaces all over the world.

This situation continues - shining a fierce spotlight on housing as it becomes clear that, while for some this has been a delight, for others it has caused substantial hardship. At the start of the pandemic, there was an expectation that things would soon settle down and "return to normal". It now seems clear that the shift to working from home is likely to be permanent in some form, and to some degree, or other. The UK Trades

---

1 ONS 2014.

2 Seetheworkhome.com and workhomeproject.org - also Holliss 2015; Holliss 2021; Holliss 2022.

3 OECD 2021.

4 ONS 2021.

5 VOXEU CEPR 2021.

Union Council found 91% of those who worked from home during Covid, want to continue post-Covid to some extent or other.[6] No matter what their occupation, or housing situation, most people do not want to relinquish the increased control over their lives that they get from working from home. This can be interpreted as a paradigm shift with major implications for the economy, for society - and for the built environment. A conversation is now underway - of which this *Home Made* exhibition is a part - that is starting to consider how to design well for this structural societal shift.

But working from home is nothing new - and neither is designing for this working practice. Before the industrial revolution almost everyone worked in their homes or lived at their workplaces, often in buildings deliberately and specifically designed for the dual purpose. Medieval homes and workplaces were inextricably linked. For the rural poor, all the activities of everyday life were carried out in and around the open-plan longhouses in which they and their animals shared space. For the urban middle-class, domesticity and business, public and private, were interwoven, with family and customers alike, eating, drinking and socialising in the central space of the merchant's house. For the wealthiest, the gentry, who inhabited substantial manor houses with their retinue of servants,

the lives of the entire household revolved around the central hall. This transformed, daily from workspace to dining room to sleeping space for most - and every few weeks into a courtroom where taxes were set, disputes resolved.[7]

Sixteenth and seventeenth century inventories from two English villages,[8] listing the occupations of the deceased and the contents of their homes, room by room, reveal almost universal home-based work - in a wide range of occupations. Most were small farmers, but the rest covered the necessities of life: mason, bricklayer, labourer, sawyer, carpenter, blacksmith, weaver, tanner, glover, tailor, barber surgeon, miller, baker, victualler, grocer, draper, butcher, inn-holder and gardener. Their homes ranged from single-roomed buildings to 22-roomed mansions, but most had four and eight rooms, at least one of which was a workspace. While "work" for most people was still carried out in and around their home, by the end of the seventeenth century it was increasingly allocated a separate space.

Weavers' houses were common in the eighteenth and nineteenth centuries, distinguishable by large windows that maximised the natural light that fell on the loom. Called "topshops" in Coventry, where they were usually positioned on the upper floor of the house (Fig. 11),

6 TUC 2021.
7 Holliss 2010.
8 Steer 1950.

they took a variety of different forms, depending on the affluence of their inhabitants. UK silk-weaving masters inhabited large, elaborate houses, often with a weaving garret on the top floor to maximise natural light. In contrast, in Switzerland and eastern France weaving cellars were placed in the basement of the farmhouse, to guarantee the humid environment necessary for working on lines, the activity shaping the architecture. The combined homes and workplaces of UK journeyman silk-weavers - who ran their own businesses employing family-members and apprentices - often juxtaposed large weavers', and domestic scale, windows. Even the cottages of the poorest weavers - to whom work was "put out", involving piecework, the delivery of raw materials and collection of the finished products - had large windows so the weavers could work all the daylit hours.

As well as the vernacular, so-called "high" architectural history also teems with buildings designed around home-based work. In some cases, these contained essential services: firefighters, for example, lived above their fire-stations until as late as the 1980s in the UK.

The 1898 Lauriston Fire Station in Edinburgh (Fig. 12), by Robert Moreham, fills an entire block, combining housing for 40 firefighters including elegant apartments for the Fire Chief and two Deputy Fire Chiefs and their families floor

Fig. 12: Robert Moreham (architect), Lauriston Fire Station, 1898, Edinburgh, United Kingdom

– and stables for the horses that pulled the early fire engines off the rear yard. In the UK, France and elsewhere, teachers lived in their schools, the police in military barracks or in police-houses behind police stations, managers lived next to their factories and, before every house had a private bathroom, bath superintendents and matrons lived in apartments within the Public Baths.[9]

Other buildings that combine dwelling and workplace (I coined the term "work-home" in 2007 to facilitate their analysis and understanding[10]) were commissioned by individuals with distinct spatial requirements. Artists' houses, with large areas of often north-facing glass to the studio (Fig. 13), were common in the late nineteenth and early twentieth centuries, especially in Paris. Ozenfant's atelier – designed by Le Corbusier in 1922 – is maybe the most famous example. Ground and first floors, accommodating garage and staff quarters, bedroom, bathroom, kitchen and "museum", are at a domestic scale, while a second-floor double-height studio has huge windows and saw-toothed rooflights to maximise the natural light. This also had semiotic

Fig. 13: Frederick Wheeler, St. Paul's Studios, 1890, Barons Court, London, United Kingdom

---

9 Holliss 2015.
10 Holliss 2007; Holliss 2015.

value – advertising the art school that sculptor Amedée Ozenfant ran there for a while. Architects have also often designed their own workhomes – in part as a way of showcasing their architecture, but also because they have the skillset to produce buildings that meet their particular spatial and environmental requirements. Notable examples include Victor Horta's 1901 Art Nouveau Brussels example, with separate, adjacent but internally connected, home and studio. The opulent entrance and stairway to the house connects to the principal's office next door so a client does not come into contact with either Horta's architectural workforce or the more utilitarian aspects of the workspace. Le Corbusier designed his own apartment in 1933 at 24 Rue Nungesser-et-Colis in Paris, to include a large studio where, on a daily basis, he painted, before going to his architectural office in the afternoon. Spatially continuous, the studio, hallway and living room were undifferentiated spatially or materially - neither function was prioritized. Ray and Charles Eames' celebrated studio-house, designed in 1949 in Los Angeles, continued this theme. Using industrial materials throughout, there was no attempt to distinguish architecturally between workplace and dwelling. Although formally divided into two buildings with a courtyard between, in reality home and work were an uninterrupted

continuum. Michael and Patty Hopkins' 1976 home and workspace in Hampstead, London, follows a similar model. When first built, the only internal partitions of this office-cum-family home were venetian blinds. The bed was in the same space as the office, and there was no acoustic separation between home and workspace.

The history of the workhome is compelling: examples can be found in every period, in every country across the globe. Such buildings are also often featured in contemporary architectural journals - particularly in Japan and the Netherlands where regulatory frameworks are more favourable than elsewhere.[11] And informal versions, made by inhabitants to meet their own distinct spatial needs, can be found in the more neglected, and therefore affordable, parts of cities across the world. In Hackney Wick and Fish Island in east London, for example, over 600 living/ working spaces were made by young creatives in disused and neglected light industrial buildings - by 2013, it was the densest concentration of artist studios in Europe.[12]

Survey after survey, post-Covid, indicates the success - for both employers and employees - of what has been termed the biggest global experiment in home-based work.[13] But dwelling and

---

11 For example: nakastudio.com/works/psh_01.html; nakastudio.com/works/m_apart_01.html; mei-arch.eu/en/projects/schiecentrale-4b/; jojanssenarchitecten.nl/project/92pc; Holliss 2015.

12 Brown 2013.

13 Holliss 2021; Coll. 2020 (B); Howard 2003.

workplace have been deliberately and systematically separated at both the building and the urban scale, since Ebenezer Howard introduced his Garden City idea, with its regrettable central spatial strategy of separating home from work, in 1903.[14] There is now an urgent need to bring them back together again, to create buildings and cities that support and encourage this popular, family-friendly, environmentally and economically sustainable working practice.

I identified a number of useful design principles in 2007, through research that analysed the lives and premises of 76 UK home-based workers from across the social spectrum in a wide range of occupations and building types.[15] The first concerns the home-based workforce itself. Today, as a result of the Covid-19 pandemic, IT based teleworkers are in the spotlight. However, in reality - as sociologist Catherine Hakim found in 1998[16] - people work from home in a wide variety of occupations, from childminder to curtain-maker, architect to academic vicar to journalist and data analyst to mechanic. Nine different groups were identified in the sample of 76, each with distinct spatial and environmental requirements.[17] Contrast those of the senior social policy researcher with two small children, for example, with the young single sculptor who, making vast constructions from rusty steel, wants to live and work with other young creatives. One of the central findings of this underlying research, therefore, is that one-size-does-not-fit-all when designing for home-based work.

A second principle concerns the nature of these buildings themselves. Three distinct types emerge when work-homes are analysed according to their Dominant Function: home-dominated, work-dominated and equal-status.[18] Put simply, some people work in their homes, some live at their workplace, while others inhabit buildings in which the domestic and workplace aspects have equal status on the street. A lack of understanding of this led to major problems on both sides of the Atlantic in the 1990s, when the idea of the "live/work unit" was developed, following its invention as living and working spaces for artists in the SoHo area of New York in the 1960s.[19] Thousands of units were built with the expectation that they would be work-dominated: workplaces with ancillary domestic usage. Instead, they were built as home-dominated – primarily

---

14 Howard 2003. In the absence of polluting industry, the spatial separation of dwelling and workplace is no longer a necessary component of the Garden City model. In the context of the debate about urban agriculture and the 15-minute-city - and if reconfigured to interweave work and home - the Garden City idea has substantial contemporary potential.

15 Holliss 2007.

16 Hakim 1998.

17 theworkhome.com/user-groups/

18 theworkhome.com/dominant-function/

19 Zukin 1988; Holliss 2015.

homes with ancillary workspace. In both east London and San Francisco this led to uproar - and changes to planning regulations - as developers made disproportionate profits on live/work projects that achieved almost residential prices having been built on (cheap) light-industrial land, by swiftly transforming employment districts to smart residential areas.[20]

The fact that most contemporary housing is speculatively built is problematic in terms of design for home-based work. This is because four inherent variables - the occupation, the nature of the household, the amount of space available and the personality of the homeworker[21] - result in often conflicting spatial and environmental requirements, including public/private, noisy/quiet, clean/dirty, safe/dangerous, etc. One thing has become clear through Covid, however, and that is that housing needs to be bigger if it is also to include home-based workspace.[22] The middle class generally achieves this through under-occupation, often having a spare bedroom, an underused dining room or a disused garage in which to create a workspace - or a garden where they can build a home office or studio. The young and the poor do not usually have this option, however. In the UK this includes a disproportionate number of people of colour,

introducing social justice as a central theme.

An emerging solution is to design housing that is larger than the standard housing product, flexible in use and adaptable over time. The terms flexible and adaptable are often used interchangeably in architectural writing,[23] but in the context of designing for home-based work they can usefully be used to distinguish between spatial changes that can be made without the need for building work - for example by opening and closing doors, sliding wall partitions etc - and those made through the use of building work, for example by demolishing or building walls, or extending a property.[24] It is currently unusual for housing to be purposely designed to be flexible and adaptable - people are instead expected to fit their lives into the spaces provided for them. This, however, becomes more difficult when work comes into the picture, because people have such different preferences and requirements.

A scheme built in Barking, east London in 2022 provides a possible model for squaring this circle. Designed for working-class artists on low incomes, in one of the poorest boroughs in London, imagination and lateral thinking lie behind both financial and spatial strategies. A House for Artists, by Apparata

---

20 LRR 2005; Parker and Pascual 2002.
21 Holliss 2017.
22 Holliss and Barac 2021.
23 Schneider and Till 2016.
24 buildingsandcities.org/insights/commentaries/lessons-adaptable-housing.html.

Fig. 14, Fig. 15: Apparata Architects, *A House for Artists*, 2021,
Borough of Barking and Dagenham, London, United Kingdom

Architects (Fig. 14), consists of a dozen deck-access apartments for artists sitting three-to-a-floor above free-to-use workspace. Although designed to Nationally Described Space Standards, a radical approach to the fire regulations - involving a secondary external fire escape balcony at each level - gives each apartment an additional 7-8m^2 by removing the need for internal corridors. Large pairs of sound-proofed double-doors in "soft spots" in party walls allow the three second floor apartments to be opened up flexibly into a single space for co-living or co-working purposes (Fig. 15);[25] the first tenants of these are collaborative theatre and performance practitioners. An elegant perimeter structural design maximises spatial adaptability in each individual apartment, allowing almost all internal walls to be removed to create an open-plan living/working space as desired. Conversely, the external skin has been designed easily to accommodate the insertion of additional internal walls to create more cellular series of spaces. Non-structural party walls can also be manipulated to make the units bigger, something taken for granted in houses where back/front/side/attic extensions are run-of-the-mill, but generally impossible in flats. Large areas of glass maximise the natural light in the apartments, echoing historic weavers' windows - these open fully onto the linear courtyard access deck, an upstand beam providing an inside/outside seat at cill height. All external spaces are designed to encourage

interactions between neighbours and the creation of community. Fundamental to the scheme is a radical approach to the public funding of the building by the local authority, which has invested its Community Arts budget in the building. The resident artists each, in effect, barter part of their week's work – to conceive, curate and deliver the Community Arts Programme - in exchange for cheap rent and free collective ground floor workspace. Exciting stuff.

The Covid-19 pandemic has permanently changed the landscape of work and, as a result, the way we inhabit our homes, buildings, streets, neighbourhoods and cities. This opens up immense potential – and an urgent need - for innovation in the way we conceive and design the built environment, better to meet the needs of contemporary society.

---

25 Holliss 2022.

1. THE HOME WORKSHOP: THE INTERMINGLING OF WORK AND PERSONAL LIFE

Introduction   43
Fabien Petiot and Chloé Braunstein-Kriegel

The chambrelans of Limoges   45
Ariane Aujoulat

Home factories: The photographic   48
investigation of Antony Neuckens around 1910
Fabien Petiot and Chloé Braunstein-Kriegel

New technologies in the home: 52
a post-industrial "relocation"?
Fabien Petiot and Chloé Braunstein-Kriegel

Exhibited works   54

Fig. 16: Rag doll, 20th century, fabrics, Industriemuseum, Ghent, Belgium (inv. V08580)

INTRODUCTION

Whether it is used for craft, manufacturing or art, or even for "making", "repairing" or "creating", the term "workshop", through its metonymy, intertwines the space it designates with its occupants, in the same way as the word "office".[1] This fusion between the individual and their environment is an expression of the ingenuity required when living and working spaces become one. It represents individuals who have to contend with the particular ergonomics of their work as they move amongst machines, materials and products.

Here we see examples of work being done in confined spaces that are both workshop and home. This particular kind of choreography has already been presented in the factory by the American sociologist Lewis Hine in his long photographic study (1908-1918) for the National Child Labor Committee.[2] The photographs show children working in cotton mills where they are able to slip between the machines to make simple repairs without production having to stop thanks to their small stature. The photographs of his contemporary Antony Neuckens[3] contain striking images of the human body in the workers' rooms[4] of industrial Belgium at the beginning of the 20th century. On entering these interiors, the photographer immediately captures the overcrowded conditions where work encroaches even onto the beds.[5] There is little or no room here for the inhabitants, who have to take up as little space as possible. Here a worker seeks out light near a window so that she can see her work more clearly. Now and again, the solitude and silence of the workshop room are broken by the song of a caged bird (healthy birds were used to check for carbon dioxide emissions) or the chatter of lacemakers on their doorsteps. Some of the photographs highlight the repetitive, meticulous nature of the work, which seems to be conducted in silence, with the workers simply communicating with an occasional furtive glance.

In the 19th century, factory owners installed looms in the homes of Lyon silk workers, who had to maintain these machines that took up all their free space. So much so that they created an architectural typology in its own right and indirectly shaped the city by forcing workshop interiors to accommodate them. An example of this is the Croix-Rousse district of Lyon. The Jacquard loom, which was introduced at the beginning of the 20th century, is about 4 metres high and determines the day-to-day organisation of the household. There is little room for anything else in the remaining space. Natural light is helpful for working in these small home factories, while the darkest corner is used for sleeping (usually an attic) and cooking. The partitioned interior is therefore organised to

---

1 See this principle applied to the office in Petiot 2016.

2 The aim of these photographs was to bring about change and reform and they went some way in changing the law on child protection. See Lesme 2014 and Goldberg 1999.

3 Askenasi-Neuckens and Galle 2000.

4 See Perrot 2009.

5 See the text dedicated to this project pp. 48-51

favour work over the well-being of its inhabitants. We generally associate workers with a factory environment. Bringing together workers and their production tools in a single factory-type space is a recent phenomenon in some cases. This is true of the tapestry sector in Aubusson (Fig. 27) from the beginning of the 19th century. Some independent weavers still work from home to this day on horizontal looms, which take up less space in their living area.

The dispersion of work naturally affects the personal living space which, even with the best possible framing and filters, cannot be completely blocked out during a video-conference. The producers in a report for French television in 1966[6] had some fun working with an unusual scene: Dr Auzoux's anatomical papier-mâché models made in Normandy, skinned and showing networks of blood vessels and nerves, standing in stark contrast alongside children's homework and a meal on the stove (Fig. 23). This may seem like a trivial example, but it is representative of this intermingling of work and private life. The same applies to these toys, rag dolls, rocking horses and skipping ropes (Fig. 32), made by parents for the children in the household using scraps from products made in the home. They provide a strong image of a living environment that was completely imbued with activity and work.

Contemporary artisans, artists and designers are familiar with this intermingling of the workshop, the office

and personal life that sometimes even involves the family. Whether by necessity or choice, freelancers do not count their hours and their freedom is relative. They often do not have the luxury of a separate work space due to property prices. Work and family routines rub along together as best they can, and sometimes support one other. The fact remains that the personal relationship that develops with the living environment inevitably spills over into the home workshop. To the point that we might wonder whether work is a member of the family in its own right as, whether we like it or not, it too takes up room in the home.

FP | CBK

---

6 *Les Actualités Françaises*, 24 August 1966 (duration: 02:02). This report on the Normandy village of Saint-Aubin-d'Ecrosville, which specialises in the production of *écorchés* for educational establishments, looks at how they are made in workshops and in the artisans' homes. The models show the networks of blood vessels and nerves.

The chambrelans of Limoges

Ariane Aujoulat,
Museum Curator, Musée national Adrien Dubouché, Limoges - Cité de la céramique, Sèvres et Limoges, France

The boundary between the industrial world and home working is not always clear. In the 19th century, the porcelain factories in Limoges were housed in old buildings that were unsuitable for industrial use. They were equipped at huge expense with machines and kilns capable of reaching the 1400°C required for the production of porcelain. However, until the beginning of the 20th century, most of them did not have complete decoration workshops: apart from the "tracers" who worked in the factories, the porcelain makers could subcontract the hand-made decorations to a network of small independent workshops and chambrelans such as Étienne Furlaud (Fig. 18), who took orders from Tallandier and Pouyat. These decorators, working in confined spaces in the home were able to obtain "muffle" kilns,[1] which were

Fig. 17: Mrs Nativité Coronat's burnishing tools, 20th century, Musée national Adrien Dubouché, Limoges - Cité de la céramique, Sèvres et Limoges, France

---

1 The muffle kiln is a small kiln used to fire painted decorations at low temperature (overglazing), once the white porcelain has been fired at high temperature (1400°C).

suitable for overglazing. They decorated items for factories, or bought plain products that they painted and sold themselves.

Some chambrelans became famous for their pâte sur pâte (paste-on-paste) decoration in an academic style. However, they were known above all for their "grand-feu" (high-temperature) glazes that characterise Art Nouveau porcelain, but which are impossible to fire in small muffle kilns. The porcelain maker Gérard Dufraisseix, who was keen on this particular technique, made his factory kilns available to chambrelans wishing to experiment.

While independence from the industrial sector had the advantage of greater artistic freedom without commercial constraints, these artists still needed financial and technical support. The "Collectivité des céramistes chambrelans" (chambrelans ceramic artists' community) was founded for this purpose in 1890, thanks to subsidies from the Haute-Vienne General Council and the Limoges City Council. It originates from a group created in 1889, allowing 44 independent artists to present their creations at the Paris Exposition. In 1901, the chambrelans community had around fifty members, thirty of whom were active, and it was even suggested that their china be marked with three intertwined Cs.

The "chambrelans community" wanted its members to perfect their art. Almost all of them had graduated from the National School of Decorative Arts in Limoges, where they had followed a course in the aesthetics of ceramic art. In 1911, Furlaud was appointed a member of the Higher Council of this school, a sign that the chambrelans had become firmly integrated into a professional network.

The attachment of this kind of production to the home environment is reminiscent of movements that aimed to promote the value of craftsmanship over industrial production, in the wake of the Arts & Crafts movement in England. For example, the chambrelans pieces on display at the 1889 Exposition are presented as being

Fig. 18: Étienne Furlaud, *Square plate (Plat carré)*, circa 1860, hard-paste porcelain, Musée national Adrien Dubouché, Limoges - Cité de la céramique, Sèvres et Limoges, France (inv. ADL 10425)

entirely handmade, "to the exclusion of any mechanical process".[2] Home-based activity was synonymous with creative freedom from the constraints of industry, and encouraged the expression of artistic personalities. The search for excellence was upheld by high-quality teaching and recognised by prestigious awards, which, alongside the distinctions gained by the factories, enabled Limoges porcelain to become famous on the national and international stage.[3]

The activity of the Limoges chambrelans is therefore defined less by their place of work than by their position within an artistic and industrial milieu. While women were in the majority in the factories, they were virtually absent from the chambrelans community, even though they were allowed to join[4]. This can be explained by the promotion of ceramic artists, most of whom were men, at the expense of home workers, who were active in the field of Limoges porcelain but worked on enamel and gold decoration. The gilding tools of Mme Nativité Coronat (Fig. 17), who worked for Haviland for 22 years before setting up her own gilding business in 1969, bear witness to this.[5]

---

2 Vogt 1901.

3 This was evident in particular, at the Paris Expositions in 1889 and 1900, where they won a gold medal, and in Chicago in 1893.

4 The association's by-laws stated that it was open to both men and women.

5 Donation of burnishing tools (2022) by Nativité Coronat (born in 1932) to the Musée national Adrien Dubouché, Limoges, France. She worked from her home for various clients, major brands (Lafarge, Bernardaud) and lesser known decorators (Malvergne, himself a subcontractor of Coquet and Michelet). The decorated pieces were usually delivered to him in baskets by his clients. She charges by the hour for the work carried out from her kitchen.

Home factories:
The photographic investigation of Antony Neuckens around 1910

Fabien Petiot and Chloé Braunstein-Kriegel

From the second half of the 19th century onwards, the notion of "travail à domicile" (home-based) work refers specifically to gainful employment carried out inside a home that has been turned into a workshop. "Unlike the craftsman, who owns his tools and is free to make what he wants and sell it to whomever he wants, home-based workers depend on a boss who provides them with the raw material to be processed in exchange for a meagre remuneration",[1] paid for via an intermediary, sometimes even in kind (exchange or "truck system"). The phenomenon is ubiquitous in Europe and North America, even as far away as New Zealand,[2] and contributes to the impoverishment of workers. The way industry was structured from the Second Industrial Revolution onwards radically transformed both trade and consumption. The invention of the sewing machine, which soon became widely used, responded to this acceleration in demand, which required an increasingly sustained rate of production. Adopted by home-based workers, it transposed the industrial principle of a streamlined production line designed for optimum efficiency to domestic sewing workshops. However, this was a transitional phase, as many products could not yet be manufactured, in whole or in part, industrially. Their diversity was based on the wide variety of skills of the different craftsmen who made them: they were specialist artisans, whose small-scale activities have now disappeared.

The circumstances may be incredibly varied (whether you want to work in the town or in the country, whether you're single or have a family, a widow or widower), but there are several common

Fig. 19: Jules Potvin, Poster for the *Travail à domicile (Working from home)* exhibition (Brussels, International Exhibition, 1910), Universiteit Bibliotheek, Ghent, Belgium (inv. BIB.AFF.C.000076)

---

1 Avrane 2019.
2 Avrane 2010; Coll. 2022.

denominators: the home-based worker is predominantly female, isolated and far removed from the systems of working-class solidarity whose members might even see her as a competitor. She is also subject to the goodwill of the intermediaries who order from her. In short, he/she is permanently shut up at home, as if cut off from the world. In addition to this, the first signs of social progress achieved thanks to new laws on working conditions, such as in France the law on health and safety in industrial establishments (1893), on accidents at work (1898), or the law establishing Sunday as a day of rest (1906), all too often stopped at the front door or the bedroom door.[3] Although Karl Marx himself described the domestic labour of the past as a "department outside the factory" and Henri de Boissieu as a "factory in the home",[4] this parallel mode of organisation would never be free and independent. It is, however, conspicuous by its absence in the struggles of the workers' movements of the second half of the 19th century. In the German philosopher's analysis, it is a victim of physically broken links with the workers' collective: "Workers' power of resistance declines with their dispersal" while "competition between workers necessarily attains its maximum".[5]

However, extensive sociological surveys were carried out at the beginning of the 20th century in several countries, mapping the living conditions of home-based workers with impressive precision.[6] These field studies make the link between work and home, which are closely intertwined and particularly damaged, at a time when poor housing was becoming a public health issue.[7] The pace of production, which was becoming ever more intense as industry progressed, had an impact on workers, including those based at home. Indeed, the range of working hours was constantly increasing and the term "sweating system" began to appear, mobilising the whole family, and first and foremost, even young children. Infirmity, contagious diseases, poisoning and insalubrious conditions were the norm in these hard-working households. The pace of work was such that the quality of production inevitably dropped, while these groups of home-based workers were swept into ever greater misery, to the extent that the world began to become aware, and it was soon a real political issue. At the turn of the 20th century, exhibitions were held in London in 1904 and in Berlin two years later, shedding light on all those who had been forgotten by

---

3 Askenasi-Neuckens and Galle 2000, pp. 35-41.

4 De Boissieu 1902.

5 Marx 1990, p. 199.

6 Examples include Charles Booth's extensive inquiry into life and labour in London (1886-1903), which is now part of the archives of the London School of Economics (available at booth.lse.ac.uk). See Booth 1902; the huge project undertaken in Belgium by the Office du Travail with 12 volumes published between 1899 and 1912; or the national studies carried out by the Office du Travail in France on female workers in the lingerie industry (1911) and the artificial flower industry, mainly in Paris (1913), cited by Perrot 2009, chapter entitled *Ouvrières à domicile*, pp. 193-199, which refers to Moret-Lespinet 2008. For the iconographic representation of home-based work, see also (*Heimarbeit*) in Germany: Denninger, Schiemann and Bitzegeio 2023.

7 The Amsterdam School cooperative workers' housing in the Netherlands, the building sites of anarchist Barcelona in around 1900, the HBM (Habitations à bon marché or low-cost homes) on the outskirts of Paris or the involvement of intellectuals such as Ellen Key (1849-1926) in Sweden responded to the influx of working-class people from the countryside into cities unprepared to receive them at the turn of the 20th century.

industrial progress. The didacticism and rigour of the second of these served as a model for subsequent events. What they revealed about working conditions was particularly moving, and resulted in the establishment of consumers' leagues (Ligues sociales d'acheteurs), and sometimes even led to legislative advances.

The case of home-based work in Belgium (15 to 17% of the population, 60% of whom were women, circa 1910[8]) is a particularly good example. The economic

Fig. 20: Antony Neuckens, *Ouvriers réalisant des reliures cousues (Workers making sewn bindings)*, circa 1910, glass plate photography, Mundaneum, Mons, Belgium (inv. ARC-MUND-DIAV-TD-055-72)

---

8 Askenasi-Neuckens and Galle 2000, p. 35.

crisis in Flanders was compounded by the crisis suffered by the linen industry in around 1840.[9] Poor harvests and epidemics wore down rural populations, who were forced to give up the freedom of an economy based on the complementary relationship between agriculture and weaving, in favour of the subjection of workers to bosses who loaned out materials and tools in exchange for very low-cost production. In Belgian socialist circles, the idea was put forward of making use of the Brussels Universal Exposition planned for 1910 (Fig. 19) to devote one of the pavilions to home-based work, and thus extend the very thorough inquiry by the Office du Travail on the subject (launched in 1899).[10] However, there are rarely any images in these inquiries, and neither do they feature heavily in exhibitions focusing on labour.

It is a pity that there is no information about how the Belgian Antony Neuckens (1875-1948), himself a glove maker and a socialist,[11] got his hands on a camera. However, he did fill a considerable gap, and in an unprecedented way. Indeed, between 1909 and 1913,[12] he set up his camera in working-class interiors, capturing the work in progress, far from the studio settings dictated by the technical constraints of the time, with fake extras and sets. Neuckens' pictures (Fig. 6, 10, 20) are sometimes blurred, the subject backlit or overexposed, but that doesn't matter: the quality of the collection outweighs any aesthetic dimension.[13] Like Eugène Atget at the same time in Paris, he established a kind of inventory. There are a multitude of weavers and lace makers, but also a wide range of trades related to metalwork (armourers), wood and plant fibres (upholsterers, rope makers, jute weavers), skins and leather (fur pluckers, glove makers), garments, packaging (those who glued paper bags together) or unclassifiable trades such as decorating confectionary and edging mourning paper. Indoors and in farmyards, in public spaces invaded by work and populated by child labourers, everyone was looking for the daylight that made work possible, sometimes under the watchful eye of a foreman.[14]

The 1910 exhibition (Fig. 19) presented Neuckens' images in a large, 400m² space, alongside a large volume of statistical data. The surrounding gardens were dotted with reconstructions of the houses of home-based workers who, the real attraction, continued to work in front of the many visitors. Despite the Sunday best worn for the occasion, the meticulous hairstyles or the freshness of the wallpaper, these stagings were faithful to Neuckens' images. Indeed, in these temporary installations, as in the photographer's pictures, it was not always possible to distinguish the workshop from the dwelling, the worker from the inhabitant, as one absorbed the other, and vice versa.

9 Scholliers and Gubin 1996.

10 See note 6.

11 On Antony Neuckens, see Askenasi-Neuckens and Galle 2000, pp. 17-33.

12 The resulting glass plates are preserved in Belgium at the Museum of Photography in Charleroi, the Ghent Archives and the Mundaneum in Mons, where we were lucky enough to have a look at them.

13 Avrane 2019.

14 "In the proto-industrial environment, the role of a foreman was limited to delivering the yarns and then collecting the woven fabrics and checking their quality" according to Jarrige and Chalmin 2008; see also Terrier 1996, p. 156.

New technologies in the home: a post-industrial "relocation"?

Fabien Petiot and Chloé Braunstein-Kriegel

The long-promised diffusion of 3D printing[1] to a wider, non-professional audience, from businesses to homes and schools, has not yet become a reality. American futurist Jeremy Rifkin championed it in the early 2010s, placing additive manufacturing at the forefront of a third Industrial Revolution.[2] This tool makes it possible above all to work towards a form of self-sufficiency which, in the strategies of certain states, may even be akin to protectionism.[3] The focus is on the industrial fabric, which is a local source of employment. Today, the use of 3D printing is still limited to the high-tech industry (aircraft parts, electronic components, car bodies, jewellery, spectacles, etc.) and the biomedical sector (hearing aids, bone prostheses).

The current crises (health, energy and climate) mean that we need to reassess things: while this *high-tech* undoubtedly has many advantages, we must not neglect certain *low-tech*, flexible and inventive solutions. This was intuitively understood by designers, those eternal troublemakers that the industry never imagined would hijack industrial tools in the early 2000s, such as those used by car designers.[4] We now need to reconsider how we use materials, as shown by numerous projects involving clay, printed ceramics and the creation of architecture, a fertile crossroads between the technique of assembly in clay coils and digital technology. The French duo Bold, on the other hand, has taken an interest in PLA,[5] thus combining the sustainability of the material with the expressiveness of the design (Fig. 21). Clear and forward-looking, the *Purity of Silk* project (2018) (Fig. 31) by Dutch artist Iris Seuren combines 3D printing and the work of silkworms: an openwork

---

1   The additive manufacturing process, i.e. the addition of successive layers of material (plastic, wax, metal, clay, etc.) was initially intended for research and prototyping for industry in the 1980s, before turning to production in the 2000s.

2   Rifkin 2014.

3   The creation of the National Additive Manufacturing Innovation Institute in the United States (an agency dedicated to 3D printing innovations) by Barack Obama in 2012, followed by the launch of the AM Forward programme included in Joe Biden's massive investment plan (May 2022), show the country's desire to repatriate certain production processes that had previously been relocated mainly to Asia. See the Additive Manufacturing Forward (AM Forward) programme, designed to stimulate the growth of additive manufacturing in the US. Supported by the government, it is based on an agreement between large manufacturers (multinationals) and their small suppliers based in the US to support workshops throughout the country, including small and medium-sized enterprises (SMEs). Link: whitehouse.gov/briefing-room/statements-releases/2022/05/06/fact-sheet-biden-administration-celebrates-launch-of-am-forward-and-calls-on-congress-to-pass-bipartisan-innovation-act/ (Accessed 19 April 2023).

4   The *Ge-Off Sphere* suspension by Ron Arad (2001, ed. The Gallery Mourmans, Maastricht, The Netherlands) was a pioneer in this joyful diversion.

5   A polylactic acid-based biodegradable polymer produced by industrial composting, through the fermentation of sugars or starch, from food waste, and here in the case of Bold's *Hairy Vases*, from wood, coconut and bamboo.

dress form bust is "colonised" by insects that produce a tangle of non-woven silk threads that clothe the figure. This installation thus moves the traditional silkworm farm, or even the workshop of the old Lyon silk manufacturers, to the side of the house where silkworms can be raised. This process does not claim to solve or counteract the phenomenon of *fast fashion* and its dramatic consequences. Here the designer proposes the home as a possible alternative to the "workshop of the world", a relocation that her project suggests rather than plans.

The home workshop, potentially an area in which hybrid technology can grow, that combines *high* and *low tech*, needs to be integrated on a global scale, because this is also what is expected of the designer, by considering the ordinary person as a stakeholder in a production and value chain. The aim is obviously not to compete with the industry, but to encourage the possibility of an alternative. The *prosumer*[6] can operate on a local scale from his kitchen, laundry room, balcony or garden. This is being encouraged by the miniaturisation of digital tools and the redesign of energy models. People are working in their own way to partially relocate certain types of production, such as customised clothing using laser cutting, the production of dyes obtained by cultivating bacteria or the printing of dishes from food waste.

Fig. 21: Bold (William Boujon and Julien Benayoun), *Poilu*, 2020, 3D printing using PLA filament filled with plant fibres (bamboo)

6 Or "prosommateur" in French. This neologism coined by the sociologist Alvin Toffler (Toffler 1980) refers to the professionalisation of a category of people who are both *consumers* and *producers*.

Exhibited works

22

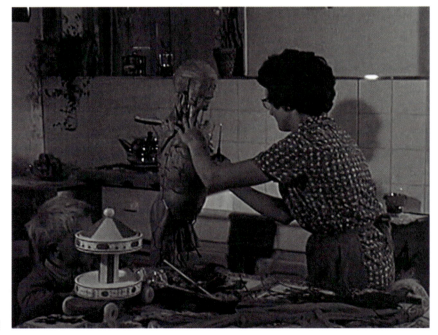

23

Fig. 22: Computer, 1982, Non-Linear Systems Inc, Industriemuseum, Ghent, Belgium (inv. V20860)
Fig. 23: *Les Écorchés de Saint-Aubin d'Ecrosville [Anatomical models from Saint-Aubin d'Ecrosville]*, 24 August 1966. Television report in *Les Actualités Françaises*, duration 02'02, INA archives, France
Fig. 24: Singer sewing machine, 20th century. Singer Manufacturing Company, Industriemuseum, Ghent, Belgium (inv. V02590)
Fig. 25: Daniel Frasnay, *Madame Régine B... fabrique en 1957 à Romans, des chaussons à domicile (Mrs Régine B... home production of slippers in Romans in 1957)*, 1957. Photograph (silver print on baryta paper, monochrome), MUCEM, Marseille, France (inv. 2004.15.9)

24

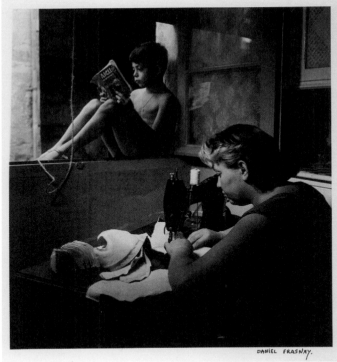

25

26 LA CRISE LYONNAISE. — Intérieur d'un tisseur en soie. — [D'après nature, par M. Férat.]

27

28

29

Fig. 26: *La crise lyonnaise – Intérieur d'un tisseur en soie*, 3 March 1877. Wood engraving after a drawing by M. Férat, paper, Collection Gadagne – Musée d'Histoire de Lyon, France

Fig. 27: Pascal Gautrand and Cédric Balaguier (direction), *La Cité de la Tapisserie 3/3 – Maudite licorne ! Marion Lozach*, 2014, video, 4'29, prod. Cité Internationale de la Tapisserie et de l'Art tissé, Aubusson, France / Institut Français de la Mode / Made in Town

Fig. 28: Denise Sussfeld, *Fabrique de gants. Ouvrières venant chercher le travail qu'elles font à domicile (Glove manufacture. Female Workers coming to collect the work they do at home)*, 1938. Photograph, MUCEM, Marseille, France (inv. Ph.1938.9.114)

Fig. 29: Hella Jongerius, *Video of the Space Loom #2* in action during the *Woven Cosmos* exhibition at Gropius Bau, Berlin, Germany, in 2021. Production: Gropius Bau and Cultureshock

57

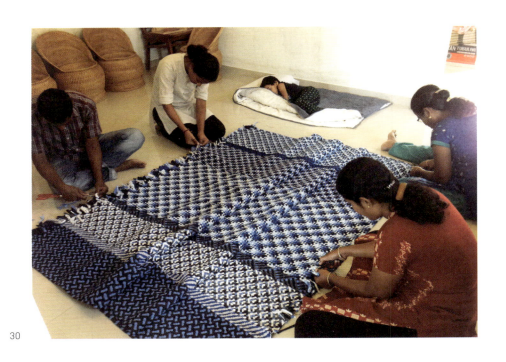

30

31

Fig. 30: Studio Brieditis & Evans, *Kasuri* (indigo version) made in India (*Re-Rag-Rug series*), 2013, cotton

Fig. 31: Iris Seuren, *Purity of silk*, 2018. Biodegradable 3D printing and silkworm weaving

Fig. 32: Skipping rope, c. 1920. Fabrics and wood, Industriemuseum, Ghent, Belgium (inv. V28851)

Fig. 33: Atelier Baudelaire x Arp is Arp x Bold Design, *Jeux de mots (Word games)*, 2020, 3D printing in PLA and PET plastic in 5 colours and varnish

32

33

2. WORKING IN THE HOME

Introduction 63
Fabien Petiot and Chloé Braunstein-Kriegel

Repairability: technological skills of ordinary people 67
Fabien Petiot and Chloé Braunstein-Kriegel

House Music, the origins of a domestic sound 70
Christophe Vix-Gras

Hair, a highly sentimental raw material 73
Antonin Mongin

Exhibited works 76

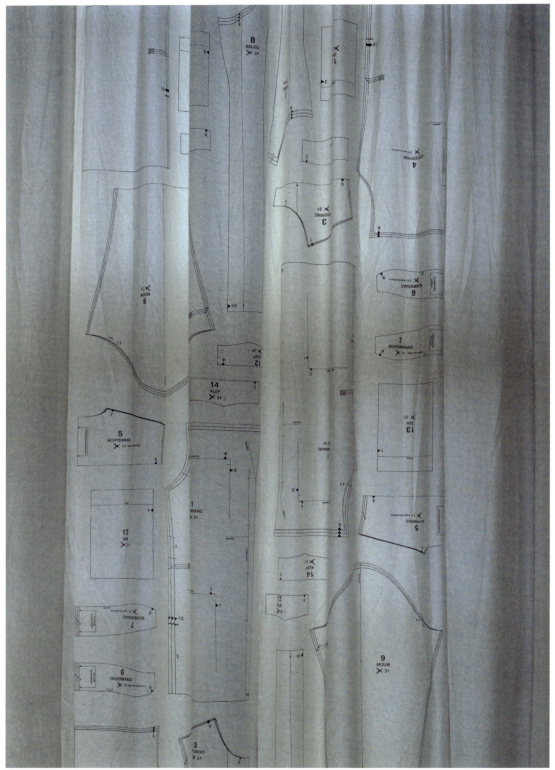

Fig.34: Djoke de Jong, *Gordijn met knippatroon (Patterned curtains to cut out)*, 1993. Printed cotton, Centraal Museum, Utrecht, The Netherlands

INTRODUCTION

It seems incongruous at first sight to our contemporary eyes to liken the simple fact of living to carrying out a profession. It is worth noting that the idea that a "housewife" said to be "without a profession" is still to this day considered to be unemployed.[1] The home has gradually become separate from wage-earning, productive activity since the second half of the 20th century. It has by and large become a place for family life, rest and recreation, rather than a place of work. The global pandemic of 2020-2021 reminded everyone of the possibilities of bringing together these two worlds with varying degrees of success.

At the same time, there have been rapid developments in recent years in domestic equipment that allow the ordinary person to compete with the most seasoned professional. A word of warning however: it is bordering on indecency to talk about the convenience, abundance and sophistication of domestic equipment and to assume that it is freely available to everyone when poor housing remains an epidemic. However we still have some shared customs and dreams that enable us to analyse this era and possible future developments, with advertising playing its part as usual in whetting people's appetite for this kind of lifestyle. Your ambitions to fit out your kitchen like a starred chef, play high-definition and 4D films in your living room, light up your headboard in hotel style or create a proper beauty routine may be more or less achievable, but they all reflect a common desire to make your daily routines more "professional". The fantasised restaurant, home cinema and personal spa are seductively transforming the living environment into a model that offers flexible à la carte services, while maintaining the appearance of a home: it is becoming like a hotel. The (symbolic) deconstruction of the home began with the arrival of desktop computers, followed by laptops, and telephones that have become mobile and "smart". Thanks to these devices, it is possible to work from any room in the home, meaning that each member of the family can be autonomous.[2] These tools are blurring the functions and symbolism of rooms that were once sanctuaries, such as the parents' bedroom for example.

Since the 2010s, this ideal has fundamentally changed our relationship to the home and its design. We might try to find the causes (as well as the aesthetic and functional models) in mass tourism, the ever-widening dissemination of decorating and furnishing trends by the media or the exponential growth of DIY shops, or we may see it as the culmination of a search, in these uncertain times, for optimal comfort, not forgetting the trend towards using interiors as spaces for

---

1 Dominici 2021; Fiori-Astier 2006; Hardyment 1988; Schwartz Cowan 1983.
2 Montjaret 2000.

reception and social gatherings. With the success of home economics and the *Ideal Home Exhibition* in the middle of the 20th century, household appliances, according to Andrea Branzi, replaced bourgeois domesticity and its "faithful servants". Since then, the widespread use of electronics in the domestic appliance sector has promoted the principles of multifunctionality and rationalisation of the modern kitchen. From the initial research in the 1930s to the emergence of connected objects, this proliferation of services has extended to every room in the house, and even to the city, explains the Italian designer.[3] In his opinion, on this scale, it is no longer a matter of developing new structures but rather or finding available spaces: "places of connection where we can live, produce, sell, exhibit, experiment and learn".[4] Wi-Fi has made it possible to work from anywhere, and co-working spaces, pop-up shops and restaurants, drives, dark stores and dark kitchens[5] all reflect this trend and are creating a new kind of urban lifestyle.

We are getting to the point where we wonder whether we really need to leave the house at all. In the 1970s, the tendency to withdraw into the home, better known as "cocooning", was a reaction

Fig. 35: Stéphane Bureaux, *Hyperbol* installation, 2015. Glass, steel and resin (galalith)

---

3 Branzi 2000.
4 *Ibid*, p. 180.
5 In major cities, these phenomena can be seen in warehouses that resemble traditional supermarkets, but without the customers, and restaurants without tables that are designed for deliveries only.

against a stressful environment (pollution, HIV, urban violence, working conditions). Is what we are witnessing now a form of bunkering?[6] With the growth of e-commerce (extension of teleshopping), socialising via social networks with no need to meet in person, distance learning and tutorials, videoconferencing, streaming platforms, online banking, etc., the role of the Internet is honing this culture of "everything from home",[7] which is open to the world whilst at the same time being enclosed, networked and intimate. By refocusing on the living environment, home working and production are creating a kind of empowerment that its creators have seized upon in imagining its implementation.

This fierce desire for independence became political with Enzo Mari's *Proposta per un'autoprogettazione* (1974) (Fig. 36, 45), a re-appropriation of the production of a whole range of furniture by the inhabitant.[8] It became critical and ecological with Thomas Thwaites' tragi-comic attempt to make his own toaster, an assembly of more than 400 components that sold for £3, from the search for minerals to the injection of plastic in his backyard...[9]

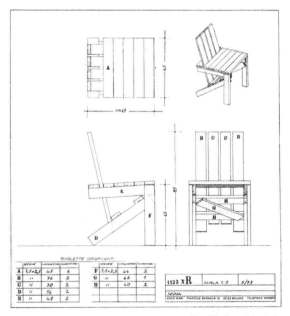

Fig. 36: Enzo Mari, *Autoprogettazione?* (Mantova, Italy: Corraini, 2002)
Plan and photograph of a chair from the series *Proposta per un autoprogettazione*, 1974, Centre de documentation, CID Grand-Hornu, Hornu, Belgium

6   The American futurologist Faith Popcorn is credited with coining both terms. See Chatenet 2020.
7   Ibid.
8   "Mari does not cultivate the myth of the good savage or tribal cults, but perhaps he thinks that we live in the megalo-necropolis of neo-capitalism like Robinson Crusoe on his island. In order to survive, he had to start making the tools that would allow him to build an environment in which he could live. Mari is right, everyone should create: after all, it's the best way to avoid being created," writes G.C. Argan, "Valutazione critico-artistica", *L'Espresso*, 5 May 1974, in Mari 2015, p. 34.
9   Thwaites 2011.

Fig. 37: Rod Hunt, *Restart Futures*, 2017

Producing in the home also involves the issue of food. Stéphane Bureaux's experimental work, based on the recipe for the first artificial polymers, culminated in the production of casein milk bowls (Fig. 35, 48), i.e. made from milk, from his kitchen. In terms of music production, the home studio is built around accessible, compact electronic equipment, so that a music studio can be set up in the home and new sounds and alternative dissemination streams can be created[10] (Fig. 39-40). In another variation on the theme of the inhabitant's know-how, the latter becomes a co-creator, as in the *Do Create* collection (2000) by the Dutch collective Droog Design (Fig. 49). The skills required are modest (hitting with a sledgehammer, scratching with a fork or breaking a vase) but they finish off the object by making the purchaser a full-fledged performing associate of the designers.

FP | CBK

10 Paris 2016.

Repairability: technological skills of ordinary people

Fabien Petiot and Chloé Braunstein-Kriegel

Mobile phones and tablets, once our pride and joy, now lie inert and dispassionate in our drawers. Out-of-date appliances are regularly banished from our kitchens, soon to be replaced by new and more efficient models. Most discarded electrical and electronic equipment contributes exponentially to the world's largest waste stream: e-waste.

We are starting to think upstream about how to make up for the extraction of virgin natural resources, known as "critical raw materials", by using recovery and recycling channels.[1] Certain components can definitely be reused.[2] But the uncontrolled accumulation of e-waste, such as in South-East Asia and West Africa, is condemning the ecosystems

Fig. 38: Luc Deriez / Repair Together, *Escape box*, 2021, wood

---

1 Waste Electrical and Electronic Equipment (WEEE).
2 In France, researchers at the CNRS are trying to develop a process that couldextract precious metals from mobile phone circuit boards (CNRS, THYMO project - Hydrometallurgical treatment of mobile phone circuit boards).

and populations of these regions a little more each day.

Whether it be in terms of versatility in fashion, outdated technology or technical failure, programmed obsolescence[3] or the wear and tear suffered by our household appliances are not inevitable. Making users more responsible and adopting a more virtuous model lead to initiatives for repairing appliances so that they can have a new lease of life instead of polluting the environment. This is the position of the international Right to Repair campaign, represented in Europe by associations such as The Restart Project. Progress has been slow, but the obligation for manufacturers to offer consumers a range of spare parts and a network of independent repairers is gradually becoming a legal requirement. [4]

Restart parties and *repair cafés* provide opportunities to learn collectively how to repair or improve appliances,and to collect useful data from the repairability movement. Conviviality and community spirit are at the heart of these events, whose aim, beyond the objects involved, is "to repair our relationship with electronics",[5] and more generally to renew the way we view objects and our consumption habits. This is the spirit in which the UK association Repair Together has designed its *Escape Box* [Fig. 38], inspired by well-known puzzle games, as a way of lifting the restraints on the process of repairing rather than discarding and replacing with new. Tutorials and open source documents also help people to develop their skills in a more personal setting. All these elements help to make ordinary people feel more professional, even though the advanced technological skills of local repairers are still undervalued.

How can we make the most of the dormant material libraries housed in our drawers, wardrobes, storage rooms, cellars and attics? It is conceivable that in the future, storage, sharing tools and training will among the services available in residential buildings. The spillover of individual space into common areas could also extend beyond the building and out into the local area. Recent initiatives in the clothing industry have taken advantage of space-saving technologies to recreate a new garment from another.[6] Innovations such as these create potential economic networks, by sourcing raw or processed

---

3 Programmed obsolescence is the set of techniques designed to reduce the life or use of a product in order to increase the frequency of its replacement. See Dannoritzer 2010.

4 Since January 2021 in France, it has become mandatory to display a repairability index for certain electrical and electronic products under the anti-waste law for a circular economy (Law n° 2020-105 promulgated on 10 February 2020). The calculation of the repairability index is based on access to documentation, disassembly capability and the availability and price of spare parts.

5 therestartproject.org/about/

6 This is demonstrated by the Garment-to-Garment Recycling System (G2G) (2018), implemented with the Looop project developed by the Hong Kong Research Institute of Textiles and Apparel (HKRITA) in collaboration with the H&M Foundation in 2020. The *fast fashion* giant presented a factory outlet in one of its Stockholm shops, a new association of textile manufacturers and major retailers. The staging is playful and spectacular, as in the installations of UNMADE (developer of software for designing and manufacturing clothes on demand) in the London department store Selfridges, or Shima Seiki (manufacturer of 3D knitwear production machines) in the stores of the Japanese retailer UNIQLO.

materials from within our own city rather than travelling to the other side of the world. However, repairing products on an individual scale is still most virtuous solution, at least in the short term, as is clearly shown in the tutorials of the Fixing Fashion association.[7] In many respects, recycling remains a mirage which unfortunately does not solve the problems linked to overconsumption, and sometimes even contributes to sustaining the use of disposable products.[8] In other words, just as it is better to turn off the tap when faced with a water leak than to bail out relentlessly, recycling cannot be the only way to solve the environmental problem as a whole.

7 fixing.fashion/index.html.
8 Berlingen 2020.

House Music, the origins of a domestic sound

Christophe Vix-Gras,
A major player in electronic music. Creator of the blog vixgras.com

Electronic music was originally studio music at a time, in the early 1970s, when avant-garde bands such as Kraftwerk and Tangerine Dream or artists such as Pierre Henry and Jean-Michel Jarre were appearing on the music scene. Digital technology then overtook analogue in the early 1980s, freeing musicians from any kind of framework, making music in a way "domestic", and then "off-piste". Music is said to be domestic because it can be made "at home" thanks to the ability of technology to reduce a multitude of instruments and effects to a single piece of software, such as Cubase (1989)[1] for example. The home studio is becoming smaller and smaller, and can now even be located on mobile

Fig. 39: Christopher Woodcock, *DJ Nicole Otero*, 2005.
Photograph from the series *Bedroom Rockers. Where Djs Call Home* series

---

1   Commodore 64 (1982), Atari ST (1985), TR 808 (1980), TB 303 (1982), Cubase software (1989) and the MIDI (Musical Instrument Digital Interface) standard (1985), all stemming from the digital innovations of their era, revolutionised music technology, among other things.

applications or tablets. All this "domestic music" can conquer the world!

In the mid-1980s, the precariousness of black American artists in Chicago and Detroit pushed a generation of pioneers to create from home, imitating James Brown or Prince without any funds behind them. Amateur DJs and musicians such as Jesse Saunders, DJ Pierre, Frankie Knuckles, Larry Heard and Farley Jackmaster Funk, used the Commodore 64 (1982) or the Atari ST (1985),[2] Roland's TB 303 and TR 808 (1980) drum machines,[3] originally intended for rock guitarists who wanted to practice at home. Legend has it that DJ Pierre was inspired by kids playing with a TB found in a bin. The beginnings of House therefore have an intrinsic link with the urban world. It is urban music, composed at home and first played in Chicago at the

Fig. 40: Christopher Woodcock, *DJ Broken Window*, 2005. Photograph from the series *Bedroom Rockers. Where Djs Call Home* series

2 *Ibid.*
3 Paris 2016.

Warehouse (or The House), a nightclub founded in 1977.

The possibility to stay at home and endlessly compose inspired the humour of the English electronic music composer Aphex Twin, who was very much inclined to stay in his beloved Cornwall, in his depiction of a "bedroom generation": "I get up in the morning, sit down and start composing in my pyjamas. And then I go back to sleep".[4] However, not all of these "musicians in pyjamas" are associated with the domestic sphere. The Micronauts, a French electronic artist, claims that "the domestic sphere has no influence" on his music. The creative setting has no major impact: an artist can procrastinate outside, (although) renting a space and working away from the home is more conducive to a healthy mental balance. "We are social animals and need to interact with others".[5] Other artists, such as Pierre Noisiez, a DJ and producer linked to the Brussels FUSE, have a different approach: "I created [a home studio] by rearranging my house into two work spaces, a studio and a library. The domestic sphere influences my creativity".[6] The private sphere does not have the same importance for all artists. For The Micronauts "the inspiration is always there, but you have to engage your brain to be creative. The location has no influence".[7]

It is intriguing to see that all urban music has a strong relationship with the places in which it is created and played, such as (former) warehouses, located in industrial areas like the Warehouse in Chicago. House is an artefact of black urban music, such as hip hop and later trap, etc., which, through borrowing (*sampling*[8]), has created its own utopia, with a sprinkling of Stakhanovites of sound evolving in an interconnected, global Tower of Babel. We can speak of a techno utopia because of the revolution in musical technology, the rise of the DJ as an artist and phonographic producer, and a futuristic imagination bathed in humanism, fraternity and love. Creativity is liberated by tools, even if the computer does not solve the problems of creativity according to Patrick Vidal, musician and DJ, pioneer of Rock and House.[9]

Music can be made more easily when you are cocooned in the place of your choice, be it in a flat or a mega-studio, or while roaming on a mobile. It is music that makes the space, and the space creates an echo for the waves and melodies.

---

4 *Ibid.*

5 Interview with the author for the catalogue *Home Made - Create, Produce, Live*, April 2023.

6 *Ibid.*

7 *Ibid.*

8 Use of existing musical extracts in new compositions.

9 Lacourte 2023.

Hair, a highly sentimental raw material

Antonin Mongin,
Textile designer-maker, researcher and writer

The art of working with hair is a craft that has been dormant since the beginning of the 20th century. It was a popular trade in the West two centuries ago in which private individuals gave their own cut hair, or the hair of a loved one, to a "hair artist", so that they could transform it into jewellery or paintings of high commemorative and sentimental value. Although we attribute its decline to photography, as a modern means of preserving individual or collective memories, historians still do not know where this practice originated. Only written documents[1] dating from the 14th century mention the existence of a custom of giving locks of hair to people as a token of affection. It was not until the 16th century that woven

Fig. 41: Antonin Mongin, pearl necklace, *Phylactères capillaires* series, 2023.
Pearls filled with the hair powder of a mother and her two daughters

Fig. 42: ring, *Phylactères capillaires à initiales* series, 2023.
Initial ring with hair powder from Christofer H.

---

1   In the *Roman de Dame Fayel*, written at the beginning of the 14th century by the poet Jakemès, the lady gives the lord of Coucy her "long blond tresses" which he wears around his helmet as he heads out to seek his fortune in the Holy Land.

hair was worn around the wrist or attached to the finger with a ring.[2] Hair was considered at the time as an expression of emotion which, once it has been cut, is made into jewellery.[3] The golden age of this practice in the 19th century owes a great deal to Romanticism. Professionals[4] operating in workshops used their know-how to make customised jewellery from hair given to them by clients. These objects were worn in times of mourning or to celebrate important life events (births, engagements, marriages) or were used in a family motif, such as a family tree. The first manuals on how to learn these techniques were produced alongside this craft activity[5] (Fig. 43, 44).

In this digital age, in which our memories are often digitalised, my research in textile design, entitled l'Artisanat d'art du cheveu coupé[6] (the art of cut hair), aims to revive and enrich this practice by restoring the commemorative value that it has lost. We also need to consider the domestic space both as the source of a material (hair) with unexpected technical qualities and as a production site. The tools used for this technique, which are often tiny as in the household appliances sector, are somewhere between the work of the laboratory technician and that of the goldsmith. The revival work that I carried out during the first lockdown in 2020 as part of the *Phylactery Capillaryproject*[7] (Fig. 41, 42), "modernises" the forms and the manufacturing process used in these types of

Fig. 43: Bracelet, circa 1860. Hair and gold. Private collection

2 Munn 1999, p. 43.
3 See the 16th century poem *Ode à un Sieur Amy* by Théophile de Viau: "There, with a passion neither firm nor light, I would have given my ardour to the eyes of a shepherdess, Whose innocent heart would have satisfied my wishes, With a bracelet of hemp with her hair."
4 An example of this France were the workshops of P. Florentin and Lucien Corné in Paris, J. Marcellin in Creil and the Maison Chevron in Troyes.
5 See the instruction manuals Munn 1999, Maribon de Montaut 1986, Celnart 1828 and Campbell 1866.
6 Mongin 2022.
7 A phylactery is a talisman (or amulet) that a person wears, containing relics of a saint (in the Catholic religion), verses from the Bible (in the Jewish religion) or sentimental bodily fragments from one's own body or that of a loved one (profane in my project).

hair products. They are always made to measure and engraved with the initials[8] of their sponsors. The successive lockdowns forced many people to consider home haircuts as a necessity for the first time, following the temporary closure of hairdressing salons. The first 3D printed jewellery contains hair fibres obtained from haircuts during or after these quarantine periods (trimming fringes, split ends and men's hair). These short pieces of hair, which are less than 5cm long (1 to 6 grammes), donated by the people I know are no longer considered as waste, but as a precious raw material which acquires a "new lease of life" with a high emotional and symbolic value.

Fig. 44: Bracelet, circa 1860. Hair and gold. Private collection

8   The initials engraved to order echo those found on certain rings, bracelets, pendants and hair brooches from the 19th century. These letters are inspired by English calligraphy, which we have modernised with the help of calligrapher Christofer Hursul.

Exhibited works

45

46

47

Fig. 45: Enzo Mari, *Chair, Proposta per un'autoprogettazione* series, 1974 - produced in 2016. Wood, collection CID - Province de Hainaut, Hornu, Belgium

Fig. 46: Humade (Lotte Dekker and Gieke van Lon), *New Kintsugi repair kit*, 2009. Epoxy glue and gold powder

Fig. 47: Humade (Lotte Dekker et Gieke van Lon), *New Kintsugi vase*, 2017. Porcelain and Epoxy glue

Fig. 48: Stéphane Bureaux, *Hyperbol*, 2015, installation, milk bowls made of casein

Fig. 49: Marijn Van Der Poll, *Do Hit Chair*, 2000. Stainless steel and sledgehammer with leather-covered tip, collection CID - Province de Hainaut, Hornu, Belgium

48

49

3. THE CONFINED TIME OF DOMESTIC SPACE

Introduction
Fabien Petiot and Chloé Braunstein-Kriegel

81

The "bricoleur", in a kind of perpetual lockdown
Fabien Petiot and Chloé Braunstein-Kriegel

84

The new Robinson Crusoes
Fabien Petiot and Chloé Braunstein-Kriegel

89

Exhibited works

92

Fig. 50: Erwan Bouroullec, *HBML Paper lamp*, 2020. Pine log and cleat, paper market shopping bag

INTRODUCTION

It is a perilous exercise to bring up the Covid-19 episode and its consequences, with the various lockdowns and people withdrawing into their homes. Has this (already) become part of past history? Does it, in the most negative sense, mark the start of the creations that emerged from it? Our relationship to work, the environment in which it takes place and, by extension, urban planning as a whole, has been turned upside down by this unprecedented crisis. In this sense, there is definitely a before and after Coronavirus.

Through our global lockdowns, we shared in a paradoxical event because it was both collective and intimate, breaking down everyone's routines and causing confusion. After all, how can we calmly face up to something that is unprecedented and stressful? Hovering between stupefaction and resignation, we became stuck in a kind of presentism and there was talk of "suspended time" for those lucky enough to find it. We found ourselves in the "rift of time" that Hannah Arendt tried to grasp in the midst of the crisis, and[1] which François Hartog has described as a "regime of historicity".[2] How can we relate to the past and project ourselves into the future when everything is a state of emergency, with curfews, travel permits, chaotic situations and endless waiting?

Nevertheless, the pandemic has been something of an eye-opener and accelerator.

People were literally forced to stay at home and some found the time to rethink their interior design as well as their personal development, which work had not allowed them to prioritise in the past. We started to consider our relationship with nature, our dependence on technology and our physical vulnerability. All kinds of intellectual projects have emerged from this myriad of individual situations in spite of the pervasive disorientation. A heightened sense of responsibility[3] has emerged towards a world suddenly seen as being on borrowed time in the context of a climate crisis that is more visible than ever. More prosaically, restricted in our movements, locked down or even quarantined, many of us asked ourselves "but what am I going to do at home?" This is the question that underpins all the work presented at the *Home Made* exhibition. How are we to *create, produce, live*, both literally and figuratively, in spaces that are often unsuited to this merging of work and personal life over a long period of time?

By setting ourselves up as teachers or amateur hairdressers, by regulating our work with daily video-conferences

---

1   See Revault 2011.

2   Hartog 2003.

3   This is the final principle explored in Hartog's work, *Ibid.*

and even by cooking, we become productive, reconnected with past knowledge and developed new skills. Masks were introduced first of all to make up for the lack of hospital equipment. The health services were quickly overwhelmed at the beginning of 2020 given the rapid spread of the disease. Sewing machines, which had been relegated to occasional use, started to make a comeback in the home. They offered an alternative to the scarce sanitary masks with an opportunity to create personal designs. The makers - this new generation of creators pitched somewhere between designers, artisans and engineers - used their initiative by introducing digital printing tools. They produced masks, and even created a whole range of protective equipment for carers including open source emergency ventilators. Examples include those developed in France by the Makers for Life collective or Club Sandwich Studio, at a time when intensive care units were stretched to their limits.[4]

Designers and architects, both salaried and freelance, also adapted to this period of tension and uncertainty. Like many other sectors, agencies had to learn new ways of working:

Fig. 51: Tom and Will Butterfield, *Chair 3 of 19*, 2020. Pine wood

---

4 Bouvier 2020.

remote team management and emulation, project management and communication with clients, creating together but separately, meeting on screen, and strengthening their presence on social networks on a daily basis often in a light-hearted way. From home-made moodboards on Instagram made by each member of the RDAI Ensemble agency (Paris), to challenges launched by the Basketclub collective[5] (Fig. 53, 61-67) to its community to invent new types of weaving, or the production and reinterpretation of chairs made of wooden slats, the only material available at the time (Fig. 51-52), it is clear that creativity creates both social connections and a melting pot of ideas. The domestic setting is definitely a place of inspiration, offering a huge source of materials to draw from.

FP | CBK

Fig. 52: Benjamin Edgar, *Tired, but Quite Optimistic*, 2020. Pine wood and acrylic paint

---

5 basketclub.world/about/ (Accessed on 16 March 2023).

The "bricoleur", in a kind of perpetual lockdown

Fabien Petiot and Chloé Braunstein-Kriegel

The hours spent at home working away by yourself, for your pleasure alone, and with what you need within reach, make the "bricoleur" one of the iconic figures of the lockdown. But unlike those who lived through the events of the Covid-19 pandemic and for whom this activity may have served as a way of letting off steam or getting away from it all, for this amateur it is an eminently voluntary choice. Many of the relationships between the inhabitant and the home can be better understood if you look at them through the lens of the history of modern "bricolage".

Fig. 53: Michael Schoner, *Basketclub - brief 16 : Shopping net*, 2021. Candy bras and metal wire structure

The French word "bricolage" (meaning manual activity or DIY) itself did not become common in the French language until the 1920s, while the verb "bricoler" appeared in around 1859. For a long time the notion of amateur or auto-didact was preferred.[1] After an initial phase in the 19th century marked by an increase in working hours and the abolition of public holidays and Sundays off, the second half of the century saw a slow but gradual reduction in working hours, particularly in France, and the re-introduction of days off. Workers' struggles later reinforced this trend. Then came the advent of leisure and time for oneself, which needed to be organised. At the same time, the appearance of a new array of "mass" entertainment and cultural attractions aimed at the working classes, perceived as dangerous[2] by the elites, fuelled a whole rhetoric demonising working-class idleness. In France and Germany, communal activities outside the home were organised. Public readings, concerts, sports, choirs, folk dancing, gardening etc., were all designed to keep workers away from terrible activities deemed to be immoral, such as drinking or, in a completely different vein, involvement in working-class militancy.[3] Individually and at home this time, amateur manual work played an important part in these working-class leisure activities. For example, educational books[4] were widely distributed, offering advice, tips and trade secrets for improving your interior or carrying out penny-saving repairs. These guides provided access to knowledge that certainly became more widespread, but which made it possible for anyone to master a huge range of artistic and artisan techniques, from the most basic to the most specialist and complex (cabinet making, tapestry, decorative ceramics etc.). Moreover, in the past as in the present, the idea of the "bricoleur" is of its time, incorporating technical and technological changes while resisting its consumerist counterpart. A keen disciple of repair work, his natural playground, in other words, the idea of leisure by necessity, he thus avoids the automatic move to buy new equipment[5] as is well illustrated by the brochures and mail-order sales of spare parts to make transistor radios, toasters or, more recently, remote controls. Nowadays, open source tutorials and manuals even allow the "bricoleur"-turned "maker" to get to grips with more hi-tech objects.

Starting towards the end of the 19th century, the by-product of the craze for creative leisure activities was a moral (or even moralistic) notion of free time, which some suspected was conducive to laziness and debauchery. After the Second World War, the mood was to reverse the values of modernism, which advocated a new way of life in the age of machines and progress: aesthetics overtook function; the virtues of a notion

---

1 Corbin 1995, p. 356.
2 See text by Didier Terrier in this volume, pp. 17-27, as well as Chevalier 1958 and Kalifa 2013.
3 Thiesse 1995.
4 Le Thomas 2008.
5 Le Thomas 2012.

of leisure that conformed to social morality replaced the "value of work"; the movement and energy of the city were transposed by the stillness of the worker concentrating on the task in hand. And rather than celebrating the professional who is guided in his practice or activity by a framework of knowledge and skills, the qualities of the amateur are extolled, offering a model of creative freedom and autonomy from the constraints dictated by the very definition of work from a capitalist point of view.[6]

The model of the "maison bourgeoise" (middle-class home) as an archetype spread widely in the 19th century and became a well-established concept. In this moralistic age, the family became the heart of the home with all of the patriarchal structure that came with it. When it came to leisure activities, the distinction between "ladies' work" on the one hand and "bricolage" for men on the other thus marked a clearly gendered division of roles. In the bourgeoisie of the time, amateur activities for women were tightly controlled and marked by a high level of misogyny. Under the guardianship of the father and then the husband, women were confined to the domestic sphere, unlike men, who were entitled to exist outside in the public sphere. Women had to spend their time

Fig. 54: Sylvain Willenz, *Table service RAZZLE*, 2023. Glazed stoneware

---

6   Knott 2011, p. 178.

on wholesome activities, steering clear of reading anything regarded as harmful or dangerous. They were kept at arm's length from any kind of professional pathway because this could generate an income, and therefore the potential for autonomy, which was regarded as incompatible with the husband's authority. Numerous publications dedicated to "ouvrages de dames" (ladies' work), a term used to describe manual activities regarded as exclusively feminine, such as needlework and sewing, focus on the decoration of "objets occupationnels"[7] (occupational objects). These activities were designed to keep their hands and minds busy and, possibly, to make their interiors more attractive. The "arts d'agrément" (literally agreeable arts), in other words music and visual arts, which were part of the education of young women from good families, had a more artistic dimension, but without any more ambition or purpose. Specialist magazines and exhibitions[8] showcased a wide range of ready-made objects to be decorated that were now available to buy. They often did not require any particular skill, but they did help pass the time. Pyrography on a surface that had already been drawn on, painting on a canvas to imitate a tapestry, an embroidery kit with the design already marked, cold enamel that doesn't have to be fired to apply to plaster objects to look like ceramics: housewives were entrusted with these industrial products to give

them something to do in their free time.[9]

These amateur activities required some specific thought on where they could be carried out within the home. If they took place in a reception room, comfort and formality pushed the function of workshop into the background, in favour of the boudoir. In the working classes at the turn of the 20th century and in the decades that followed, the Singer sewing machine became retractable: it disappeared into its own table and took on the appearance of a small, decorative chest of drawers with an elaborate metal base. Furthermore, the proliferation of more practical, lightweight creative leisure kits did not require a specific location for women, who therefore had to make do with a pre-existing space. In contrast, men set up ad hoc spaces for their workbenches, which were deemed to be more sophisticated. But even for these "real bricoleurs", the lack of space led to an indulgence in one-up-manship when it came to camouflaging the workbench, which could be dismantled or retracted, like one of the ludicrous contraptions depicted in William H. Robinson's cartoons (Fig. 69, 80) or in Buster Keaton's films. Turning the usual gendered practice on its head, the workshop/sofa promoted by Sam Brown[10] in 1953 meant that it was the man's turn to hide their work space, while remaining faithful to the image of the clever "bricoleur". Indeed, the carpenter's workbench

---

7 Coppens 2010, p. 105 cited by Rouen 2020, p. 32.

8 It is worth mentioning two exhibitions dedicated to art by ladies, the *Exposition des Arts de la Femme*, organised by the Union Centrale des Arts Décoratifs (Central Union of Decorative Arts) in 1892 and 1895.

9 Rouen 2020, pp. 38-40.

10 Brown 1953, pp. 48.

swivelled on itself to become an elegant upholstered seat, revealing nothing of its secondary function.[11] On another note, the garage was becoming bigger, particularly in the United States after the war, which meant that it could be deployed as a backdrop for manly know-how, becoming an almost mythical space, cultivated by those in the know, in which IT and entrepreneurial genius could thrive in the 1970s. This is the case with what was later referred to as Steve Jobs' Apple Garage:[12] the garage belonging to his parents' house in Los Altos [in Silicon Valley] became the fantasised birthplace of every start-up worthy of the name, thus turning a simple carport into one of the ultimate hotspots of contemporary mythology.

What we mean today by "bricolage" has little to do with the autodidacts and "leisure out of necessity" [repairing, saving money etc.] that it referred to until the 1960s-70s.[13] The pretext of personalisation, the last possible link with the old model, was even ultimately replaced by the standardisation of everything offered by big brands, which hold on to the word "bricolage" in name only. The concept of the "bricoleur" can often be seen in the approach taken by designers, with whom they still have some close links. However, designers only hold on to certain aspects of the term, the amateur approach stimulating their creative process.[14] And so by making their tentative

first attempts to find different forms, they learn by doing, to such an extent that they see the construction of the model as a project in its own right. This is the case of the work of the Basketclub collective [Fig. 53, 61-67], a series of challenges shared on Instagram with a community of designers keen to rediscover weaving and basketry techniques during lockdown. So both amateurs and designers appropriate artisan and industrial production tools: it is a way for them to emancipate themselves from a restrictive framework, enhancing their expressive freedom, and putting the enjoyment of making something right at the heart of their approach.

---

11 Knott 2011, pp. 162-163.

12 Galluzzo 2023.

13 The aptly chosen English term, "Do It Yourself" will meanwhile take on a political dimension that takes us away from the home, and therefore from our subject. See, for example, Crawford 2010.

14 See Petiot 2012; Coll. 2015.

The new Robinson Crusoes

Fabien Petiot and Chloé Braunstein-Kriegel

Solitude, destitution and having to deal with an unprecedented, even inhospitable, context proved an almost initiatory ordeal for Robinson Crusoe on both a physical and mental level. It was through his ingenuity and his ability to improvise that the famous castaway from Daniel Defoe's adventure novel (1719) emerged stronger from this accidental return to nature. The story is obviously a metaphor, but its lesson continues to resonate in the wake of crises, whether they concern the economy, health or the environment.

Like Defoe's hero, whose island experience leads him to try to rebuild a semblance of society as he knows it, and to concern himself with his own well-being, even to the point of governing the world he recreates *ex nihilo*, some have experienced the Covid-19 lockdowns like Robinson on his island. Once the basic necessities of daily life have been taken care of, he gradually improves and enriches his living environment, adapting it to his desires by using local resources. He successively takes on the roles of inventive handyman, farmer and animal breeder.[1] We know how the story goes, with this utopian construction slipping away from its creator along with the certainties that he had clung to in order to survive. Continuing in this vein, Andrea Branzi defended in the early 1980s the notion of "Second Modernity" and of a contemporary primitivism: "we would be like those who, having fallen out of an aeroplane in the middle of the Amazon, find themselves operating with technologically advanced elements still on board, as well as with natural materials from the forest."[2] Neither survivors nor survivalists, we are now faced with the question of how to strike the right balance between growth, consumerism, advanced technologies and access to natural resources, given the climate crisis and the inevitable scarcity of raw materials. Rather than the grand doctrines and the myth of progress, a celebration of improvisation or what has been called "ad hocism"[3] is gradually taking over from other models. It is no longer a question of low-tech or high-tech, but rather of a new kind of Robinson Crusoe. We have all experienced this during the lockdowns of 2020 and 2021, when we were confined to our apartments and had to make do with what we had, both in terms of space and objects, and in terms of time-scales.

---

1 We are referring here to the isolated Robinson Crusoe who has to grapple with his environment, and not the one who, in the course of the story, becomes a civiliser reminiscent of a colonialist. This latter interpretation is important, but it takes us away from our main subject.

2 Branzi 1986, p. 23. Gaetano Pesce also spoke metaphorically when he said: "Creating art today is like coming home late at night, when the shops closed and you have to prepare a nice dinner with what you have at home" (Pesce 1986, p. 26).

3 Jencks and Silver 2013.

The designer Erwan Bouroullec did not wind down his activities, but refocused and renewed them, accommodating the daily life of the family and a new working environment, just like Robinson Crusoe. In a house in Burgundy that is usually uninhabited, he has to make furniture so that the children can work. Varnished wooden panels recovered from the side of a cupboard are used as a desk top that rests on willow branches cut from the surrounding countryside. There is also a stool and a bedside lamp made with the children from a tree stump, a piece of wood and a paper bag. These rough assemblies, in which the branches are neither straight nor squared, reflect the urgency of creating furniture without any mechanical tools. We also see the perfect balance of furniture created by a seasoned designer and his love of plants. Bouroullec makes the hut more attractive by using natural products and assembling his findings, somewhere between Robinson Crusoe and childhood games.

Fig. 55: Erwan Bouroullec, *Impossible N1*, 2021. Sublimation printing on textile, marouflé on aluminium, Musée des Arts décoratifs et du design, Bordeaux, France

Fig. 56: Erwan Bouroullec, *SEB-LG-F71 HIMD tool*, 2020. Douglas pine wood and willow branches

Exhibited works

57

58

Fig. 57: Christian van der Kooy, *Space in the Doubt - Covid 19 The Hague 01*, 2020, photograph
Fig. 58: Hella Jongerius, *Shadow view from Woven Windows* series, 2020. Paper, linen, cotton and various threads woven on a digital Jacquard loom and epoxy-coated metal frame
Fig. 59: Studio Brichet-Ziegler, *Paper Lamp - Suspension 1 version*, 2012, paper and cardboard. Produced as part of Manufact'home ("Manufacto, la fabrique des savoir-faire", a project by the Fondation d'entreprise Hermès, Paris).
Fig. 60: Rive Roshan and Ava Paloma de la Rive Box, *Just behind the clouds*, 2020. Digitally printed high pile rug

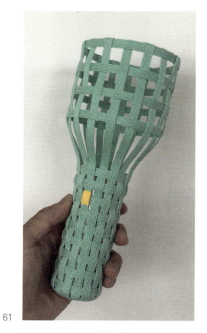

61

62

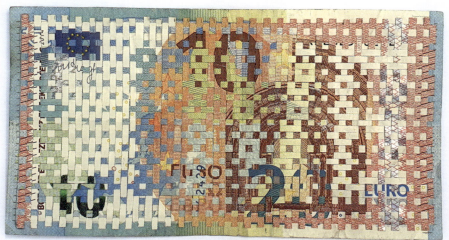

63

Fig. 61: Shigeki Fujishiro, *Basketclub - brief 10 : Lamp*, 2020. Paper
Fig. 62: Carole Baijings Studio for Design, *Basketclub - brief 11 : Paper bin*, 2020. Metal, leather, fabric and polyester tape
Fig. 63: Simone Post, *Love over money - Basketclub Brief 9 : Money*, 2023. Weaved counterfeit banknote
Fig. 64: Rein Reitsma, *Basketclub - brief 24 : Candle*, 2021. Woven candles (paraffin)
Fig. 65: Bertjan Pot, *Basketclub - brief 13 : Apricot*, 2020. Fabric
Fig. 66: Adrianus Kundert, *Basketclub - brief 16 : Sun*, collaboration with Dedon, Germany, 2021. Polypropylene
Fig. 67: Slinky Light, *Basketclub brief 10 : light bulb*, 2020. Polypropylene and PET weaving, and LED lighting

64

65

66

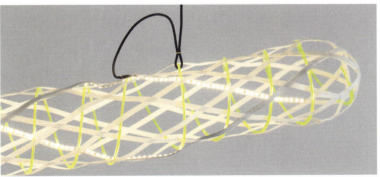

67

4. THE BUILDING, A "MACHINE FOR LIVING IN"

Introduction
Fabien Petiot and Chloé Braunstein-Kriegel

99

The "model apartment", or the emergence of new domestic landscapes
Fabien Petiot and Chloé Braunstein-Kriegel

101

Architectural modularity: the *à la carte* home
Fabien Petiot and Chloé Braunstein-Kriegel

104

Collective housing, an augmented habitat?
Fabien Petiot and Chloé Braunstein-Kriegel

107

Exhibited works

110

Fig. 68: Wald (Flavien Menu et Frédérique Barchelard), *Proto-Habitat*, 2020.
Installation in a public garden, Bordeaux, France

INTRODUCTION

From the "insulae" of ancient Rome to the first skyscrapers in Chicago in 1870, followed by those of the modernist period from the 1930s to the 1960s; from Haussmann's tenements in Paris to the international experiments of the 1960s and 1970s, the apartment block is about much more than how many floors or how tall the building is. Freeing up space on the ground, it was designed to respond to the demographic boom and the concentration of populations in cities. From an architectural point of view, it must in principle offer its occupants protection and comfort, while from an urban planning point of view, it must be integrated into the neighbourhood and the city in which it is built. Most often divided into flats linked by communal areas that the inhabitants share with varying degrees of happiness, the apartment block is much more than an architectural object or a multi-storey house.

A real "machine for living in", according to Le Corbusier's famous words, heralding a functional, mechanical approach to architecture,[1] the apartment block also provides a portrait of an era, encapsulating its aspirations. Today, it is expected to be reversible and even genetically modifiable.[2] It is a *hub*, the meeting point between the resident and their neighbourhood. Like a living organism, it can be seen as a set of networks and services. It can also be the location or medium for a utopia. And so the dream of a building designed according to the principle of the phalanstère[3] (a self-contained dwelling) or the familistère[4] was speculated upon and put into practice in the 19th and 20th centuries, and is now resurfacing in a whole new way. It is based on something that the Cités Radieuses[5] had already experimented with, providing the structure for a wide range of shared services and facilities (cultural, commercial, educational, sports, recreational, sanitary), and homes adapted to the size of different families, between generously sized communal areas. In fact, the apartment block crossed by a "street-corridor" as in the Unité d'habitation de Firminy (1967), the "vertical village" or the "community house", is designed to contain communal services and public spaces that give it a certain level of autonomy in how it operates.

However, we know that a certain inward-looking attitude quickly caught up with a world based on self-suf-

---

1 *A house is a machine for living in, just as an armchair is a machine for sitting in* (Le Corbusier 1977, p. 73).

2 Chessa 2018. Material databases, for example, managed with the help of artificial intelligence, are designed to optimise the way buildings are used and repaired.

3 A utopia dreamt up by the French philosopher Charles Fourier (1772-1837), the "phalanstère", or phalanstry in English, (a contraction of "phalanx" and "monastery") is like a small city where the buildings are designed to encourage community living among its inhabitants.

4 Inspired by Fourier, the French industrialist Jean-Baptiste Godin built the Familistère de Guise (Aisne, France) between 1859 and 1884, a housing estate for 2,000 inhabitants near his cast-iron stove factory. This "Social Palace" is one of the most ambitious social experiments in industrial history, and was in use until 1968 as a cooperative association of capital and labour.

5 Le Corbusier designed five *Cités Radieuses* in France and Germany: Marseille (1947-1952), Nantes Rezé (1953-1955), Briey-en-Forêt (1956-1963), Berlin (1957), Firminy (1959-1967).

ficiency that was responding to the needs of an era. But does this Corbusian way of living fit in with today's aspirations, which seem to lead the inhabitant towards their own environmental awareness? The flourishing of remote working can pave the way for new opportunities here: cohousing, urban agriculture, environmental sustainability, architectural reversibility and urban regeneration... How, on the basis of these febrile notions, can the apartment block become a laboratory for how we will live together in the future? Individualism, the desire for privacy[6] and the increasing autonomy of inhabitants, partly conditioned by the standardisation of the dwellings preferred by modern tastes, do not exclude some form of conviviality.[7] Lastly, the cramped conditions of the dwellings – the source of many sarcastic caricatures (Fig. 69, 80) – is driving us to spill outwards, from the balcony to the roof, via the communal spaces, just like the garden cities of the past, which were both nourishing and convivial. In the background, there is more pressure than ever: with climate change on the one hand, and the scarcity of resources on the other. Bringing work back into the thought processes of the architects who design the building means re-imagining the conditions for a more collective, or even more communal, life that does not prevent people from continuing to nurture the privacy of their own homes.

FP | CBK

Fig. 69: William Heath Robinson, *Top Floor Chicken Farm*, 1933. Reproduction of an illustration, pen and watercolour. The Heath Robinson Museum, London, United Kingdom

6 Serfaty-Garzon 2005.
7 Illich 1973.

The "model apartment", or the emergence of new domestic landscapes

Fabien Petiot and Chloé Braunstein-Kriegel

The history of interior design is closely linked to the search for the right balance between public and private spaces. This arrangement is subject to the uses and means available to the inhabitants according to their place in the social hierarchy. From the distribution of rooms in a town house,[1] to the quasi-sanctuary of the bedroom or bathroom that we know today, the layout of the home is based on issues relating to functionality. It also responds to the values of a society at a particular time in its history.[2]

The principle of the model apartment, an open space presented to the public as a template, has become the showcase for these developments. It was already ubiquitous at events such as the Salon des Artistes Décorateurs in 1925 in France, where Ruhlmann presented his "Pavillon du collectionneur". The Universal or "International" Exhibitions played a key role in this staging of everyday life, such as the "Maison du jeune homme", presented in Brussels in 1935 by the trio Charlotte Perriand, René Herbst and Louis Sognot. Whether they are luxurious or, on the contrary, more of a social enterprise, these different layouts should certainly be seen as some kind of manifesto. But, more prosaically, they are quite simply used to promote the real estate developments in question. Extensively photographed and covered in the media,[3] these model interiors have an ambiguous connotation: snapshots of their era and its aspirations, they are also reminiscent of the museographical, and so artificial, device of the *period rooms*[4] that appeared in the 18th century. But after the period of post-war reconstruction, as "mod cons" became more widespread, a new generation of architects and designers appeared in the 1960s. They wanted to do away with the mentalities of the past which they believed led to war and its disasters. This new approach was based on the rejection of the modernist myth which, in the inter-war period, celebrated a new way of life based in particular on a belief in progress.

The exhibition entitled *Italy: the New Domestic Landscape*, curated by Emilio Ambasz at the MoMA in New York in 1972, is an exemplary expression of these new attitudes, marking a turning point in the fields of architecture and design during this period.[5] By entrusting a dozen designers such as Ettore Sottsass Jr.,

1 Gady 2011.
2 Eleb-Vidal and Debarre-Blanchard 1999.
3 Colomina 1994.
4 Labrusse 2018.
5 New York 1972.

Gae Aulenti and Gaetano Pesce with the task of designing a space in the manner of a model apartment, the curator of this exhibition was keen to speak to a young generation in search of new lifestyles. In line with the ideas of the post-1968 era and the self-proclaimed "Anti-design" movement,[6] these architect/designers took a holistic approach to architecture and design that prioritised the individual and the quest for freedom, above and beyond aesthetics, function and social norms. In this vein, the spaces were organised as agoras, where lifestyles

Fig. 70: Joe Colombo in collaboration with Ignazia Favata, *Total Furnishing Unit*, 1972. Illustration from *Italy: The New Domestic Landscape* catalogue of MoMA exhibition (New York, 1972)
The Museum of Modern Art Library, New York, United States (inv. 300062429_0183)

---

6 Anti-design emerged in the 1960s in Italy and encompassed groups such as Design Radical, Archigram and Superstudio. They embraced colour, decorative touches and kitsch, regarded as impure by disciples of a more modernist, dogmatic style. Iconoclastic, experimental and often political, the movement contributed to that period's reflections on post-modernism.

were based more on leisure than on the importance of social status and its trappings. These radical positions were combined with an environmental awareness and a critical attitude towards consumerism and work as potential sources of alienation.

Italy: the New Domestic Landscape was organised into two parts: "Objects" and "Environments". The exhibition approached them from the perspective of the most radical experimentation rather than from a commercial point of view. Set up in the gardens of MoMA, most of the installations were set free from any architectural context. They were presented as autonomous, ultra-functional capsules[7] that could be multiplied at will, like the cockpits of a spaceship.[8]

Mobile homes, container furniture and micro-environments like Joe Colombo's *Total Furnishing Unit* (Fig. 70): these concepts were part of the standardisation of the home, using rotomolded plastic modules. Space is divided according to different functions (cooking, sleeping, washing, socialising), while the furniture becomes nomadic architecture (on wheels, connectable, stackable, or extendable, like the accordion-like corridors that lead passengers from the airport to the plane). A sense of urgency seems to unite what should well be referred to as a shelter, right in the middle of the Cold War. The small size means

that space must be optimised, so the kitchen is converted into a workshop, for example, and the bedroom into a mini-cinema.

---

7 Midal 2003.

8 At the same time in France, the Plastiques de Bourgogne company, working with the designer Maurice-Claude Vidili, was developing housing units such as the *Sphère d'isolement* (1970) or the *Gélule R.T.L.* office. Here again, we were flirting with an aerospace aesthetic, at once detached from the weight of the world and withdrawn into its solitude.

Architectural modularity: the *à la carte* home

Fabien Petiot and Chloé Braunstein-Kriegel

It seems quite obvious to look at the home as something other than just a place to sleep, at a time when we no longer talk about a family, but rather a "domestic group",[1] when the elderly are leaving the family set-up, and even towns and cities, and in an era when the environmental impact of buildings is becoming a crucial issue. Another significant trend that is emerging, is that work is increasingly becoming an integral part of the home. The health crisis finally rendered an urban model obsolete: a model that has been organised according to zones with only one function, inherited from Modernism. This has highlighted the current difficulties involved in changing our dwellings quickly to better suit emerging lifestyles and needs.

Urban experts, in particular urban planners, architects and designers, have long been opposed to urban policies (gentrification, vacant corporate headquarters) that all too often they see as disastrous. These policies not only exclude the

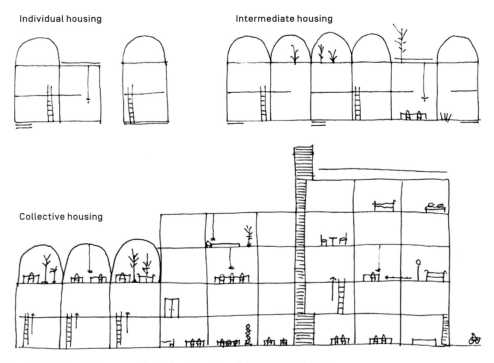

Fig. 71: Wald (Flavien Menu and Frédérique Barchelard), *Proto-Habitat*, 2020.
Drawing - Module assembly system

---

1   "Groupe domestique" in French, Eleb 2021.

working classes from city centres, but are also based on an incorrect assumption, with major consequences for towns and cities: the reduction of the domestic space to a single function, dedicated to rest and nothing else. Generation Y, the so-called "millennials", triggered the upheaval we are experiencing today in their relationships with work, consumerism and what we will call liveability. But it's the 15-25 year-old generation Z, used to choosing everything "à la carte", from their playlists to their studies to their wardrobe, for whom the very principle of ownership and, its by-product, debt over several decades, makes no sense. They prefer values linked to nomadism or collective initiatives. These young people no longer seem to believe in the promise of a better future than that of their parents. The crises, whether health, ecological, economic or social, have reinforced this worry, and many people can see pertinent alternatives in the idea of sharing spaces.[2]

In response to these emerging needs, the housing crisis and the negative effects of the urban sprawl, the principle of reversibility is increasingly favoured by urban stakeholders and decision-makers, even though the regulatory framework is still restrictive when it comes to this type of project related to the architecture of dwellings. Reversibility is a truly forward-thinking strategy for the whole city, where buildings are designed to adapt over time to the most diverse situations, to changes in lifestyles and to crises, be they health-related or environmental. This flexibility in urban planning also makes it possible to avoid the pollution associated with the unfortunate cycle of demolition and

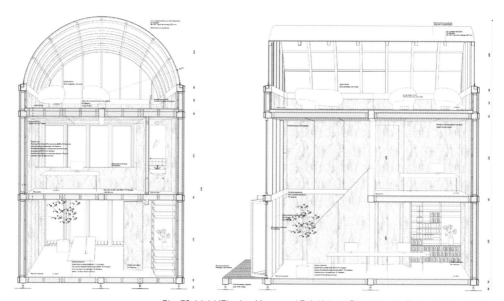

Fig. 72: Wald (Flavien Menu and Frédérique Barchelard), *Proto-Habitat*, 2020. Drawing - Sectional view of the structure

2 Gonauer 2002.

reconstruction, on which the process of change of use or conversion is generally based. However, reversibility is not to be confused with the renovation of existing buildings and spaces, which architects have long known how to do. It is therefore a question of anticipating and optimising all the different ways a building can be used in a long-term strategy of course, but also by distinguishing between day-time and night-time activities in the same architecture. Finally, it means taking into account how lifestyles, living and working conditions evolve, as well as the carbon footprint of the construction industry, by bringing it back (reuse has a long history[3]) into the concept of the circular economy. For example, by treating a building as a bank of materials that can be replaced and re-used over and over again, as in the case of the Triodos Bank headquarters (Zeist, the Netherlands) by RAU Architects and Ex Interiors, which is described as "the first large-scale 100 per cent wooden, remountable office building".

There is a lot of wood in *Proto-Habitat*, a project that serves as an articulate manifesto for the architects at the French agency Wald (Fig. 3, 68, 71-72). By striving to reconcile what they call the "three ecologies of living: social, mental and environmental", Flavien Menu and Frédérique Barchelard, two of Wald's architects, have explored the history of working from home, taking a particular interest in the types of architecture used in work-dominated homes, particularly among Huguenot watchmakers. They

reflected on the issue of the high-end rental market, which is particularly prominent in Switzerland and Germany where access to loans is facilitated for housing cooperatives. This research, during a residency at the Villa Medici in Rome, led to the *Proto-Habitat* project, a constructive system that is flexible and sustainable by nature. Locally sourced and the result of an in-depth understanding of forestry, wood plays a sensory as well as a functional role here (thermal and acoustic comfort). The *Proto-Habitat* is prefabricated, and can be assembled and taken apart in 5 days. It is made up of modules that can be used in a wide range of environments (dense or open, urban or rural): one day it's a workshop or an individual home if you add an extra floor, then transformed into something else, with a business on the ground floor and flats upstairs. Each module has an upper room that cries out to be reinvented as a winter garden, an office space or a guest room. It is the culmination of the flexibility of a habitat that is regarded as a hybrid, multifunctional space.

In design as in architecture, the idea of modularity is undoubtedly one of the most important leitmotifs of the 20th century. If the health crisis showed how feasible it could be, in an emergency, to put it into practice, the environmental upheavals to come and the new needs of remote workers/inhabitants are forcing towns and cities, as well as businesses and developers, to completely rethink how buildings are used more generally.

3   Paris 2014.

Collective housing,
an augmented habitat?

Fabien Petiot and Chloé Braunstein-Kriegel

British cartoonist W.H. Robinson (Fig. 69, 80) derided the very serious rationalisation of the modernist interiors of his time,[1] thus highlighting the capacity of their inhabitants to appropriate their environment and to find their place in the building as a whole. Weegee's photographs of 1930s New York also come to mind, with his sleeping subjects fleeing the stifling heat of their apartments, cramming themselves into fire escapes and rooftops.

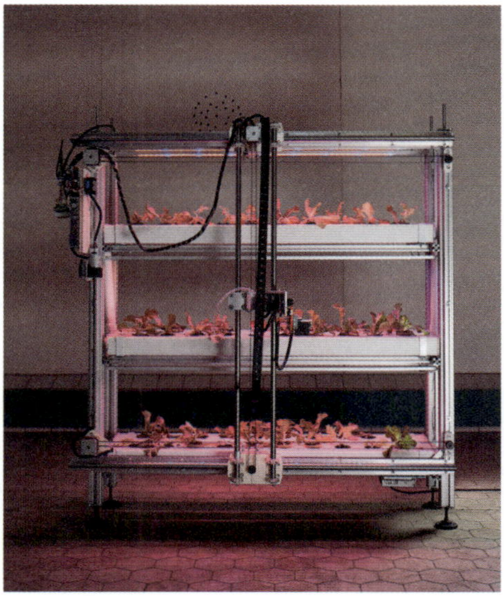

Fig. 73: Marco Federico Cagnoni, *Plastic Culture*, 2022. Steel and electronics

Prohibited because it is obviously too risky, this unauthorised use of public spaces is now taking on another form. Following the lockdowns associated with the health crisis (picnics, barbecues, gardens and gyms were improvised in communal areas), but also in view of climate change,[2] buildings are adapting to new practices. A family vegetable garden and shared chicken coop, a jointly managed art gallery or open-air cinema are all extensions that are breathing new life into the visions of the mischievous English cartoonist. Working and producing in an apartment building can now be part of the architect's brief. This is the case in France, for example, with the low-carbon social housing building, Le Candide (Cité Balzac, Vitry-sur-Seine, 2012) by Bruno Rollet. More recently, we might think of the Symbiose building (2022) by Claas Architectes in Nantes, a renovation project that included an energy-producing greenhouse, or the cooperatively designed social project, Ferme du Rail (2021) in Paris by the Grand Huit architectural cooperative: a loggia, workshop and vegetable garden are all intermediary, shared spaces. The transitional space between private spaces and communal areas, they are dedicated to both productivity and leisure. Above and beyond the issue of the building itself,

---

1 Robinson 2021.

2 The Climate Mobilization Act (2019) passed by the New York City Council calls for the installation of wind turbines, photovoltaic panels and green roofs on the city's roofs. See Eventually Made 2020.

these shared spaces give communal living an appealing sense of conviviality. A technical, sustainable infrastructure supports the whole project, freeing up the roofs and basements for other functions (horticultural greenhouse, aquaponics, mushroom farm). The same applies to alternative agriculture projects involving building façades. In this vein, the *Vertical Plastic Farm* (2018), an exploratory project dreamt up by the designer Marco Federico Cagnoni (Fig. 73, 74), presents a way of growing plants that are both a source of food and a source of bioplastics. If it were to be implemented in an urban setting,[3] this vertical farm could make the most of species (dandelion, chicory or salsify) that are both highly nutritious and packed with latex, and therefore biodegradable natural polymers, which are particularly interesting against the back-drop of a post-oil plastics industry. The robotic, digitally controlled modules are attached to the walls of buildings and maintained by the inhabitants themselves, who thus become "prosumers". In this scenario, which encourages self-sufficiency, the

Fig. 74: Marco Federico Cagnoni, *Vertical Plastic Farm*, 2022. 3D modelling

---

3 Paris 2018.

inhabitants are both producers and consumers, and can produce small bio-sourced plastic objects using domestic 3D printers.

Empowering inhabitants in this way means that we can rethink a neighbourhood's whole ecosystem. The building itself becomes a gigantic source of materials, like the city itself, which is seen as a mine of raw materials by the Belgian collective Rotor and its architectural reuse projects. In the same way, the residents' metal waste is recycled with the Ciguë agency's "pocket foundry" (Fig. 75, 76), or Emma Cogné's *Turboramas* (Fig. 77, 78), in which PVC sheaths are cut and woven into partitions that punctuate the space, forming colourful hangings. Individual to start with, the work spills out beyond the living areas and feeds into collective architectural revamping projects. This is the case of the Granby Workshop, a decorative and utilitarian ceramics workshop founded in 2015 by the architectural collective Assemble in Liverpool (Fig. 81, 82). Since 2013, the workshop has been helping the residents of a run-down neighbourhood who have formed a community joint ownership organisation,[4] committed to converting empty homes into affordable housing. The workshop produces architectural ceramics (tiles, handles, fireplace surrounds etc.), all of which are unique and the result of happy accidents

in the production process, and which are used in the renovation of houses that have long been abandoned.

Another solution involves grafting on to or "accessorising" the existing architecture, when dwellings cannot be built in their own right due to lack of space. In his *Manifeste pour une architecture insurrectionnelle* (1968),[5] Jean-Louis Chanéac argued in favour of creating "parasite cells" on the façades of buildings that the inhabitants, keen to expand, could develop themselves. In the same vein, more recently, the Dutch duo Rianne Makkink and Jurgen Bey have offered to isolate themselves right in the middle of the communal areas of apartment buildings. Their *Work At Home #3* (2013) (Fig. 79), a desk designed on a micro scale, is positioned on the steps of a wide staircase: between a hut and an extension of the private space, the workplace is once again part of the construction of a home.

---

4 *Granby Four Streets CLT*. Following in the footsteps of Wald City, it is worth pointing out the extent to which architectural inventiveness is also making its mark in the legal world, by making the most of innovative provisions such as BIMBY (Build In My BackYard), the OFS (Organisme Foncier Solitaire), which provides housing for the disadvantaged, the BRS (Bail Réel Solidaire, which distinguishes between the land and the buildings on it), temporary urban planning projects (temporary occupation of public or private spaces) and gap sites (empty spaces that are of no interest to property developers).

5 Chanéac 2005.

Exhibited works

75

76

Fig. 75: Ciguë, Melting furnace, 2019. Steel
Fig. 76: Ciguë, *Lampshades*, 2019. Cast aluminium
Fig. 77: Emma Cogné, *Turborama Grand et Petit Store*, 2018. ICTA sheath (polypropylene) and polypropylene rope. Collection CID - Province de Hainaut, Hornu, Belgium
Fig. 78: Emma Cogné, Pipe guillotine, 2021. Plywood, kitchen knives, hardware

Fig. 79: Studio Makkink & Bey, *Work at Home #3*, 2013, prototype. Multiplex oak, perspex window, aluminium with canvases
Fig. 80: William Heath Robinson, *Bedroom comfort*, 1933. Reproduction of an illustration, pen and watercolour. The Heath Robinson Museum, London, United Kingdom

80

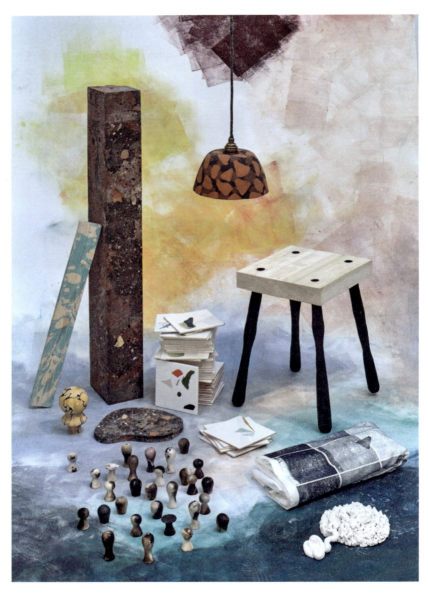

Fig. 81: Assemble, *Granby Workshops* production, 2015. Ceramics and furniture
Fig. 82: Marie Jacotey, *Granby Workshops*, 2015, drawing

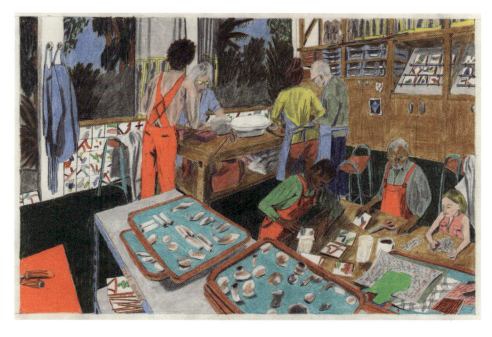

Fig. 83: VeloCity, *Growing Villages Differently*, 2017, drawing

WHEN WORKING FROM HOME SHAPES THE CITY AND THE LANDSCAPE

Fabien Petiot and Chloé Braunstein-Kriegel

There is a theme that runs through this publication: home is not an autonomous entity, cut off from the outside world, all the more so when work sets the pace for all or part of our day-to-day lives. Bringing work into this body that is our house, a space with a subtle combination of emotion and function, is no mean feat. However, it reveals the plasticity of the home. From the home studio to the nightclub, from growing vegetables to 3D printing bioplastic cutlery, from cutting a lock of hair to creating a sentimental piece of jewellery from which it's made: many situations describe the plurality and constant spillover of what we produce at home into the outside world.

Self-sufficient or – in extreme circumstances – under lockdown but still connected, inhabitants are like a *Baron in the Trees*,[1] Cosimo, the hero of Italo Calvino's philosophical novel, who, at the age of twelve, decides to live in the trees for the rest of his life: while he may well be outside the world, paradoxically he remains even more attentive and connected to it. Has the bed become our branch, a special place where we can work, read and write, socialise or keep in touch with our com-munity? A place where you can eat your meals, make love, watch TV, buy things online, even compose music, like the aptly named *bedroom pop*.[2] Lounging around, the horizontal[3] inhabitant can be everywhere at once, both physically at home, and present elsewhere at the same time, the ultimate example of the phenomenon that began in the wake of the 1973 oil crisis. "Industrialisation brought with it the eight-hour shift and the radical separation between the home and the office or factory, between rest and work, night and day. Post-industrialisation collapses work back into the home and takes it further into the bedroom and into the bed itself," writes Beatriz Colomina.[4]

The very definition of "chez-soi" (French for "home") has inevitably been transformed, or at least reworked. More than just the four walls of a house, it usually encompasses an emotional attachment, a feeling of safety and comfort. It is a completely personal transposition of oneself, without necessarily being weighed down with optimum comfort, nor justifying itself with long-term occupation.[5] What relationship do we have with our home, when

---

1 Calvino 2017.

2 "Galvanised by Tiktok, young independent artists are enjoying worldwide success with songs tackling the most personal of subjects composed and broadcast from their bedrooms. The hugely popular bedroom pop playlist is also a musical genre that extols the virtues of authenticity. A bedroom, a microphone and Garage Band software. This is often how bedroom pop artists start their career" (Bossavie 2022).

3 "I am a completely horizontal author. I can't think unless I'm lying down, either in bed or stretched on a couch and with a cigarette and coffee handy" declared Truman Capote (Capote 1957), quoted in Colomina 2018.

4 *Ibid*.

5 Coccia 2017.

work occupies the heart of the household? When we are travelling the world from the hollow of our bed? When the home is like a collection of services connected to a building or a neighbourhood? The English language explains this tension between two states very well, as summed up by architectural theorist Reyner Banham in 1965: *A Home is not a House*.[6] Producing at home, whether objects or knowledge, implies reflecting on how habitable a place is, in other words, the fragile equilibrium between functionality and privacy.

From the spoon to the city[7] via the countryside

The impact of working from home on one's immediate environment is considerable. This is true for example, with the spread of the *flex office*,[8] which some think will become the norm in the service industry. This hybrid way of combining working remotely and working on-site demonstrates the profound, worldwide change currently underway in our relationship with work and home, but also more broadly speaking with the city. The geographical dispersion of workers, the growing amount of space taken up by work in the home and the more flexible organisation

of working time led urbanist Carlos Moreno[9] to come up with the concept of the "15-minute city", which has since proliferated. Liberated from an urban planning approach previously dictated by the car, this manifesto-based model is based on a range of local services accessible by walking or cycling within 15 minutes of home. These services include education as well as leisure, health, shops and work. According to its advocates, its implementation by urban planners would help to create a poly-centric city and, on a smaller scale, a neighbourhood with a more vibrant economic and social energy. This would mean that the boundaries of the home would extend out to the neighbourhood, forcing us to rethink transport networks, but also architecture. These are expected to be versatile, reversible, sustainable or self-sufficient, in other words, efficient and adapted to the needs of the residents. Wald is following the same principles with the *Proto-Habitat*, which can be assembled and taken apart within a few days (Fig. 3, 68, 71-72). Others incorporate mixed-use programmes, such as the vegetable growing scenario of the *Vertical Plastic Farm* (Fig. 73, 74) by Marco Federico Cagnoni, or are based on the close link with the neighbourhood and the city, as

---

6 "When your house contains such a complex of piping, flues, (...) antennae, conduits, freezers, heaters - when it contains so many services that the hardware could stand up by itself without any assistance from the house, why have a house to hold it up?" (Banham 1965, p. 70).

7 "Dal cucchiaio alla città" (From the spoon to the city) was the slogan of Italian architect and theorist Ernesto Nathan Rogers in the 1950s, probably inspired by Hermann Muthesius and his "Vom Sofakissen zum Stadtebau" (from sofa cushions to city-buildings) which, in 1911, was then used as the plan for the Deutscher Werkbund.

8 This approach to management thus encourages the employee to become nomadic. Indeed, the *flex office* involves replacing an individual office with a multitude of working areas. Depending on the day, it can change from an open space to a meeting room, from a co-working area to a living room. Remote working plays a huge part in this way of working. For businesses, it's about getting round the issue of low occupancy rates for offices (which are no longer used as much due to remote working, assignments outside the office, holidays, reduced working hours, illness, and of course COVID-19) and the resulting costs.

9 A theory devised in 2015, the concept is developed in Moreno 2020.

Fig. 84: Collective project *Kilómetro Zero* led by Sanna Völker
Marta Ayala Herrera Studio, *2/1 Bench*. Pine wood; Turbina studio, *Future Archeology*, 2021. Mayolica fired clay, stone cast; Isaac Piñeiro Studio, *Sabu Bench*, 2020. Laminated wood and solid wood furniture

in the *Granby Four Streets* programme led by Assemble in Liverpool (Fig. 81, 82).

The *Kilómetro Zero* project (2020) (Fig. 84) led by Sanna Völker, a designer based in Spain, is a fantastic example of this focus on what is local. During the 2020 lockdown, when travel was limited to a radius of 1km around the home, she invited other designers to work and produce according to her guidelines, drawing on the savoir-faire available within the neighbourhoods of Barcelona and Madrid. While some were able to consolidate existing relationships, others took the opportunity to discover the rich opportunities that surrounded them, experiencing a "stronger connection with the inhabitants of their neighbourhood and the positive effects of mutual support and community."[10] Both production and deliveries had come to a halt at that time. Up to this point, the workshop of a ceramicist, a locksmith, a carpenter or an upholsterer would have blended into the background of formerly industrious suburbs. Now they have become venues where close links are forged, and even platforms for improvisation capitalising on whatever materials are available.

Interdependence between residents
Nurturing these collaborations, led at a local level, could contribute to various forms of urban resilience, as long as they can prosper. This phrase reminds us of an aptitude that allows a city and its residents to come to terms with the shock of a crisis (sudden natural disas-

ters or gradual climate change for example), and even anticipate it, rather than having to confront it.

Sadly, climate change is not showing any signs of stopping, although recently nature did show that it could (temporarily) reassert itself in towns and cities during the Covid-19 pandemic. While by 2050, urban concentration will affect 70% of the world's population, it's hard to extol the virtues of newfound proximity and remote working if heat islands or flooding make living conditions so difficult, against the backdrop of energy and food crises.

Fully incorporating home working within the urban ecosystem also means considering the roll-out of ambitious, resilient city plans. Consider for example the *Doughnut Economy* model that Kate Raworth[11] came up with. The British economist has developed an urban strategy whereby nobody is left behind, in which everyone contributes to an ecologically sustainable plan. The resilience presented by a model like this explicates the approach taken by Amsterdam, a pioneer in this area. The city is imagining itself in the post-pandemic world, striving for a fully circular economy by 2050. The municipal authorities have set themselves the long-term ambition of sharing and upcycling, available to as many people as possible. In such a network of innovative initiatives, might designers, makers and craftspeople once again find their place in the heart of the towns and cities from which they have gradually been expelled from over

---

10 Sanna Völker, in conversation with the authors on 15 February 2022.
11 Senior Associate at Oxford University's Environmental Change Institute and author of the book Raworth 2017.

Fig. 85: Studio Makkink & Bey, *Water School 4+ project (duckweed)*, 2021

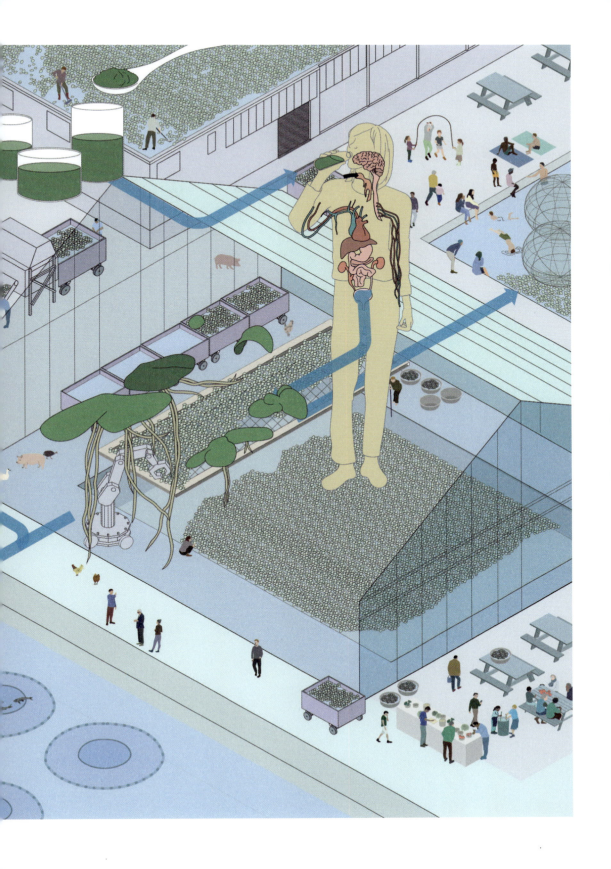

the course of the last few decades? What role do the residents have in this economy, a constellation of businesses focusing on repair, optimisation and personalisation?

This concern for the urban landscape and the environment is also shared by design and architecture studio Makkink & Bey, with the WaterSchool,[12] launched in 2012 (Fig. 85). By bringing together projects led by designers, artists, engineers and scientists through workshops and educational programmes, this project aims to rethink our relationship with water, how it is managed, and the risks of shortages. More generally, it is about reassessing our relationship with nature within an urban context. This relationship would be geared towards an economic model and the development of better living conditions. The International Architecture Biennale Rotterdam (IABR) in 2018 gave the WaterSchool the opportunity to establish itself in the Merwe-Vierhavens area (M4H+), a port site set to become home to approximately 6,300 people (residents and employees). Plans are still being explored when it comes to water consumption, as well as the carbon footprint and how it is calculated thus bringing together businesses, government bodies and designers. The production of food and energy, as well as the design of working environments, are outlined in the specifications for this urban plan, which also gives a prominent role to living organisms. For example, certain aquatic plants help filter water and provide protein for both human and agricultural consumption. Against this backdrop, where sustainability and urban resilience are key, home workers will have their own part to play, contributing to the economic model as well as to the maintenance of this new landscape.

These different examples highlight the interdependence between residents and producers. As a reminder, those who worked from their own homes in the past formed a network which may not have had the same kind of solidarity as that forged on the factory floor, but it did form a link between the suppliers of raw materials, home workers and customers, on a regional, even national scale. As part of this system, some farmers became cutlery makers, toy producers or textile workers during the off season. Meaning they diversified, guaranteeing a steady income, a far cry from the ultra-specialisation of the post-1945 productivist approach to agriculture. We see a similar theme in the second half of the 19th century and up until the 1930s: the idea that bringing electricity to the countryside and the widespread availability of motorised equipment would put an end to production in factories, bringing work into homes in rural areas, and rediscovering the multitude of activities specific to proto-industrialisation.[13] Back in the 1910s, anarchist and theorist Pierre Kropotkine even foresaw the establishment of cooperatives, bringing together producers and consumers.[14] These days, it is the quasi absence of high-

---

12 To use the definition put forward by architect Rianne Makkink and designer Jurgen Bey, the WaterSchool concept is "a speculative school designed and organised around water as an essential material, subject and social and political phenomenon". See website: smb-waterschool.nl/en/hom (Accessed on 14 April 2023).

13 Engelhard 1934; Beltran and Carré 2016, pp. 134-136.

14 See Pierre Kropotkine, second edition of *Champs, Usines et Ateliers* (1910) quoted in Beltran and Carré 2016, p. 136.

speed broadband, or what is known as the "digital divide" that continues to isolate certain regions, holding back workers keen to leave the city.

A return to the countryside

Until the second half of the 20th century, green belts around cities provided food for large and medium-sized conurbations. The end of this system not only helped to establish a geographical, but also cultural, divide between rural and urban communities.

But what exactly do we mean by "countryside"? Often the reality is far from homogenous. Some areas have been deserted because of poor access and a lack of jobs. Then there is *rurbanisation*[15] with the *ex nihilo* establishment of suburban housing estates. All of this is against the backdrop of industrialised agriculture. However, futuristic experiments have also been developed in countryside areas that would give *smart cities* a run for their money. The teams working for Dutch architect and urbanist Rem Koolhaas, along with a number of academics, have carried out research around the world into this often-ignored landscape, for the exhibition *Countryside, The Future* (2020).[16] From China to Qatar, via Siberia, Japan, the American Midwest and the Netherlands, the countryside appears to be a testing ground, a response to climate change, the growing population, ecosystem preservation or welcoming ref-

ugees. Digital technology and the use of satellites, the establishment of soilless crops, or the large-scale planning encouraged by political powers are tackling the urgency of simultaneous situations like food crises, soil erosion and overpopulation. And as the name of this exhibition suggests, they are anticipating a future with plenty of challenges.

This event turned things upside down by helping to change the way we had previously perceived the countryside. It encouraged a great deal of thought, including that of the British urbanists involved in the *VeloCity* project (2019)[17] (Fig. 83, 86). This speculative idea put forward a way of organising a territory that focuses on a new 21st century village design. Home working plays a key part in this project, whereas it is usually linked to the urban environment. Facing the abandonment of villages in the English countryside, which poses a threat to their picture-postcard image, the aging population, the disappearance of local services and rural areas that no longer constitute employment catchment areas, families and young people are reluctant to settle there. To respond to this, *VeloCity* aims not to urbanise the countryside, but rather to incorporate some of its qualities in an all-encompassing programme. It encompasses many different interdependent solutions, ranging from cycling to building design: the creation of new transport networks by reclaiming old footpaths

---

15 A French neologism created by Bauer and Roux in 1976, this phenomenon refers to the rampant urbanisation of rural spaces, the interweaving of rural spaces with urban areas, in a process also referred to in French as "mitage".

16 Koolhaas 2020. Case studies in Siberia, Japan, Kenya, the United States, The Netherlands and Qatar, for example, have contributed to the thought processes of Rem Koolhaas and Samir Bantal, director of AMO, the Office for Metropolitan Architecture's (OMA) think tank, alongside universities around the world.

17 VeloCity (A) and VeloCity (B). See also Sarah Featherstone, "Infrastructure and Placemaking", in Coll. 2020 (A), pp. 208-235.

Fig. 86: VeloCity, *Growing Villages Differently*, 2017, drawing

connecting villages; freeing up spaces (roads, carparks) once car dependency has been reduced; healthy, intergenerational, cohesive architectural projects; and the development of a shared micro-economy. Traditional architecture and landscapes are maintained, contributing to the flourishing of home working that ultimately fits in with these rural clusters. Rather than contributing to the urban sprawl, the urbanists working on *VeloCity* are relying on a distributed workforce to reshape rural areas.

When the never-ending city stretches from the urban centre to the surrounding countryside, living spaces are redesigned, no longer as a simple home, but as the setting for a more conscious, responsible relationship between inhabitants and their environment. This also involves somehow relocating professional activities. Indeed, while production workshops began to move away from urban centres in the early 20th century, we are now seeing the reverse. We may not be talking about a real ground swell, given the limitations imposed by real estate, but this phenomenon benefits from the recent success of computer-aided design (CAD) and its digital tools: they take up less space than traditional industrial machines, as well as being more affordable, thus blurring boundaries. These new tools are promoted by the makers. This new generation, encompassing all sorts of profiles, from designers, artists and artisans to engineers, geeks and amateurs, are gradually carving out their place in the heart of the urban ecosystem. Ideally, in the urban design plans of the future, production workshops, from this one at home, to that one in the neighbourhood, will offer services that could help to re-design town centres where areas dedicated to consumerism still dominate. If we are now talking about a city that is available at home, will this dissemination of doing things for ourselves help make us see the urban space around us as an extension of our home?

BIBLIOGRAPHY

PRIMARY SOURCES

Beecher 2008
Beecher, Catharine, and Stowe, Harriet Beecher [2008]. *The American Woman's Home, or, Principles of Domestic Science.* Carlisle [Mass.]: Applewood Books. [Originally published in 1898].

Beecher 2009
Beecher, Catharine [2009]. *A Treatise of Domestic Economy: for the Use of Young Ladies at Home, and at School.* Charleston [South Carolina]: Bibliobazaar. [Originally published in 1840].

Brown 1953
Brown, Sam [1953]. *Planning Your Home Workshop.* 2nd ed. Chicago: Popular Mechanics Press.

Booth 1902
Booth, Charles [1902]. *Life and Labour of the People in London.* London: Macmillan and Co.

Calvino 2017
Calvino, Italo [2017]. *The Baron in the trees.* Translation from Italian by Ann Goldstein. Boston: Mariner Books. [Originally published in 1957].

Campbell 1866
Campbell, Mark [1866]. *Self-Instructor in the art of Hair Work, Dressing Hair, Making Curls, Switches, Braids, and Hair Jewelry of Every Description.* New York/Chicago.

Celnart 1828
Bayle-Mouillard, Elisabeth-Félicie, known as Celnart, Elisabeth [1828], *Manuel des Demoiselles, ou arts et métiers qui leur conviennent et dont elles peuvent s'occuper avec agrément.* Paris: Roret.

Chanéac 2005
Chanéac, Jean-Louis [2005]. *Architecture interdite.* Paris: Éditions du Linteau.

De Boissieu 1902
de Boissieu, Henri [1902]. L'usine au logis à Paris. *Questions pratiques de législation ouvrière et d'économie sociale*, November 1902, pp. 321-326.

Howard 2003
Howard, Ebenezer [2003]. *To-Morrow: A Peaceful Path to Real Reform.* New commentary by Hall, Peter, Hardy, Dennis and Ward, Colin [Eds.]. Cambridge: Cambridge University Press. [Originally published in 1898].

Mari 2015
Mari, Enzo [2015]. *Protesta per un'autoprogettazione.* Milan: Corraini. [Originally published in 1974].

Maribon de Montaut 1986
Maribon de Montaut, Louis [1986]. *Manière de travailler en cheveux.* Paris: A. Chanlot. [Originally published in 1816-1822].

Marx 1990
Karl Marx, Karl [1990]. *Capital. Volume I: a critique of political economy*, Chap. 15: "Machinery and Modern Industry", Section VIII: "Revolution Effected in Manufacture, Handicrafts, and Domestic Industry by Modern Industry". Translated from German by Ben Fowkes. London: Penguin books [Originally published in 1867].

Robinson 2021
Robinson, William H., Coudray, Jean-Luc [text] and Merlet, Isabelle [colour] [2021]. *Survivre chez soi. L'art du confinement.* Paris: Michel Lagarde. [Originally published in 1936].

Thwaites 2011
Thwaites, Thomas [2011]. *The Toaster Project, or a heroic attempt to build a simple electric appliance from scratch.* New York: Princeton Architectural Press.

Vogt 1901
Vogt, Georges [1901]. *Exposition universelle internationale de 1900 à Paris. Rapports du jury international. Classe 72: céramique.* Paris: Imprimerie nationale.

SECONDARY SOURCES

Askenasi-Neuckens and Galle 2000
Askenasi-Neuckens, Anne and Galle, Hubert [2000]. *Les derniers ouvriers libres de Belgique.* Waterloo: Luc Pire.

Avrane 2013
Avrane, Colette [2013]. *Ouvrières à domicile.*

Le combat pour un salaire minimum sous la Troisième République. Rennes: Presses universitaires de Rennes.

Avrane 2019
Avrane, Colette (2019). Les conditions de travail des ouvrières à domicile révélées par des photographies: le cas de l'exposition universelle de Bruxelles de 1910. *Images du travail, travail des images*, pp. 6-7. Available at: journals.openedition.org/itti/700 [Accessed 25 April 2023].

Avrane 2010
Avrane, Colette (2010). *Les ouvrières à domicile en France de la fin du XIXe siècle à la Seconde Guerre mondiale. Genèse et application de la loi de 1915 sur le salaire minimum dans l'industrie du vêtement*, Angers: University of Angers, History PhD thesis.

Banham 1965
Banham, Reyner (1965). A Home is Not a House, *Art in America*. vol. 2, pp. 70-79.

Barth 2022
Barth, Isabelle (2022). Derrière la question du télétravail, le véritable enjeu n'est pas la distance, mais le temps. *Le Monde*, 8 July 2022, p. 29.

Barraud 2014
Barraud de Lagerie, Pauline (2014). L'éternel retour du *sweating system* ?, *L'Homme & la Société*, pp. 193-194, pp. 73-90.

Bauer and Roux 1976
Bauer, Gérard and Roux, Jean-Michel (1976). *La rurbanisation ou la ville éparpillée*. Paris: Seuil.

Beltran and Carré 2016
Beltran, Alain and Patrice Carré (2016). *La Vie électrique. Histoire et imaginaire (XVIIe - XXIe siècle)*. Paris: Belin, pp. 134-136.

Berlingen 2020
Berlingen, Flore (2020). *Recyclage: le grand enfumage. Comment l'économie circulaire est devenue l'alibi du jetable*. Paris: Rue de l'échiquier.

Bossavie 2022
Bossavie, Brice (2022) Home studieux. La bedroom pop cartonne dans nos playlists.

Libération, 25 February 2022. Available at: liberation.fr/culture/musique/home-studieux-20220225_5KSMFK YJC 5F47G-2J2ERNMHXPTY/?redirected=1&redirected=1 [Accessed 12 April 2023].

Bouvier 2020
Bouvier, Pierre (2020). Respirateurs, protections pour les soignants... : l'impression 3D mobilisée contre le coronavirus. *Le Monde*, 31 March 2020. Available at: lemonde.fr/planete/article/2020/03/31/respirateurs-protections-pour-les-soignants-l-impression-3d-mobilisee-contre-le-coronavirus_6035086_3244.html [Accessed 21 April 2023].

Branzi 1986
Branzi, Andrea (1986). We Are the Primitives. *Design Issues*, vol. III, no. 1, Spring 1986, pp. 23-27.

Branzi 2000
Branzi, Andrea (2000). Disparition et retour des serviteurs fidèles. Translated from the Italian by Marie-Claire Llopès, exh. cat. Paris 2000, pp. 161-164.

Brown 2013
Brown, Richard (2013). *Made in HWFI: the Live-Work Collectives*. London: See Studio.

Capote 1957
Hill, Patti (1957). Interview with Truman Capote, Truman Capote: The Art of Fiction No. 17. *The Paris Review*, No. 16, Spring-Summer 1957.

Cayez 1981
Cayez, Pierre (1981), Une proto-industrie décalée : la ruralisation de la soierie lyonnaise dans la première moitié du XIXe siècle. *Revue du Nord*, 248, pp. 95-103.

Chatenet 2020
Chatenet, Emmanuelle (2020). Le cocooning de demain. *Bilan* (online), 15 July 2020. Available at: bilan.ch/opinions/emmanuelle-chatenet/le-cocooning-de-demain-1. [Accessed 24 February 2021].

Chessa 2018
Chessa, Milena (2018). Des immeubles génétiquement modifiables. *Le Moniteur*, 9 March 2018. Available at: lemoniteur.fr/article/des-immeubles-genetiquement-modifia-bles.1953854. [Accessed 21 April 2023].

Chevalier 1958
Chevalier, Louis (1958). *Classes laborieuses et classes dangereuses à Paris pendant la première moitié du XIXe siècle*. Paris: Plon.

Cholet 2015
Cholet, Mona (2015). *Chez soi: Une odyssée de l'espace domestique*. Paris: La Découverte.

Clarisse 2004
Clarisse, Catherine (2004). *Cuisine: recettes d'architecture*. Paris: L'Imprimeur.

Coccia 2021
Coccia, Emanuele (2021). *Philosophie de la maison*. Translated from the Italian by Léo Texier. Paris: Payot.

Coll. 1981
(coll.) (1981). *Industrialization Before Industrialization: Rural Industry in the Genesis of Capitalism*. Translated from the German into English by Beate Schempp. Cambridge/New York: Cambridge University Press.

Coll. 2013
Terrier, Didier, Maitte, Corine and De Oliveira, Matthieu (2013). *L'entrepreneur et l'historien. Deux regards sur l'industrialisation dans le textile* (XVIIIe-XIXe siècle). Villeneuve d'Ascq: Septentrion University Press.

Coll. 2018
(coll.) (2018). *Work, Body, Leisure*. Rotterdam: Het Nieuw Instituut.

Coll. 2020 (A)
(2020) *RETHINK Design guide – Architecture for a postpandemic world*. London: Royal Institute of British Architects/Routledge.

Coll. 2022
Nilsson, Malin, Mazumdar, Indrani and Neunsinger Silke (Eds.) (2022). *Studies in Global Social History*, vol. 45: "Home-based Work and Home-based Workers (1800-2021)", Leiden/Boston: Brill.

Coll. 2020 (B)
Banjo, Shelly, Yap, Livia, Murphy, Colum and Chan, Vinicy. (2020). Coronavirus Forces World's Largest Work-From-Home Experiment. Bloomberg, 2 February 2020. Available at: bloomberg.com/news/articles/2020-02-02/coronavirus-forces-world-s-largest-work-from-home-experiment#x-j4y7vzkg. [Accessed 27 April 2023].

Colomina 1994
Colomina, Beatriz (1994). *Privacy and Publicity. Modern Architecture As Mass Media*, Cambridge (Mass.): The MIT Press.

Colomina 2018
Colomina, Beatriz (2018). The 24/7 Bed. Marina Otero Verzier, ed. *Work, Body, Leisure*, published on the occasion of the exhibition at the Dutch Pavilion of the Venice Architecture Biennale, Rotterdam/Stuttgart: Het Nieuwe Instituut/Hatje Cantz. Available at: work-body-leisure.hetnieuweinstituut.nl/247-bed. [Accessed 14 April 2023].

Coppens 2010
Coppens, Marguerite (2009). Le tricot manuel au XIXe siècle : d'un "ouvrage de dame" de deuxième choix vers le vêtement de mode, *La Maille. Une histoire à écrire*. Proceedings of the study days organised by the Association française d'étude du textile. Troyes, 20-21 November 2009. Marguerite Coppens (Ed.), AFET, Brussels and Paris, 2010, pp. 105-139.

Corbin 1995
Corbin, Alain (1995). Les balbutiements d'un temps pour soi. In Alain Corbin (Ed.), *L'avènement des loisirs*. 1850-1900. Paris: Aubier, pp. 324-371.

D'Aveni and Venkatesh 2020
D'Aveni, Richard A. and Venkatesh, Ankush (2020). How to Make 3D Printing Better, *Harvard Business Review*, published 25 September 2020. Available at: hbr.org/2020/09/how-to-make-3d-printing-better. [Accessed 9 April 2023].

Denninger, Schiemann and Bitzegeio 2023
Denninger, Viktor, Schiemann, Jenny and Bitzegeio, Ursula (2023). Von der Heimarbeit ins Homeoffice - eine Foto-Labour-Story. Available at: fes.de/themen-portal-geschichte-kultur-medien-netz/geschichte/ausstellungen-1. [Accessed 26 April 2023].

Eleb-Vidal and Debarre-Blanchard 1999
Eleb-Vidal, Monique and Anne Debarre-Blanchard (1999). *Architectures de la vie privée : Maisons et mentalités, XVIIe-XIXe siècles*. Brussels: Archives d'architecture moderne (Modern Architecture Archives).

Eleb 2021
Eleb, Monique (2021). Imaginer l'avenir de l'habitat: du Pan 14 et de l'Europan 1 jusqu'à

aujourd'hui. In Sabri Bendimérad [Ed.]. *Habitat*, Paris: École Nationale Supérieure d'Architecture Paris-Malaquais, pp. 125-156.

Engelhard 1934
Engelhard, J. [1934]. Ce qu'on peut attendre de l'électricité rurale. *Le Génie rural*, November 1934, pp. 21-22.

Eventually Made 2020
[2020]. Eventually Made, New Top City, *MONU*, no. 33: Pandemic Urbanism, Autumn 2020, pp. 48-53.

Faytre and Le Goff 2022
Faytre, Ludovic and Le Goff, Tanguy [Eds.] [2022]. *Fragiles métropoles. Le temps des épreuves*. Les Cahiers de l'Institut Paris Région, no. 179. Paris: PUF.

Fiori-Astier 2006
Fiori-Astier, Liliane [2006]. Les femmes au foyer : objectivation et subjectivation d'une invisibilité sociale. Doctoral thesis in sociology, under the supervision of Liane Mozère. Metz: Université de Metz.

Frame Lab 2022
Frame Lab [2022]. Mobility Hubs, *Frame*, no. 144, January-February 2022, pp. 128-131.

Gady 2011
Gady, Alexandre [2011]. *Les hôtels particuliers de Paris, du Moyen Âge à la Belle Époque*. Paris: Parigramme.

Galluzzo 2023
Galluzzo, Anthony [2023]. *Le mythe de l'entrepreneur. Défaire l'imaginaire de la Silicon Valley*. Paris: La Découverte.

Goldberg 1999
Goldberg, Vicki [1999]. *Lewis W. Hine: Children at work*, Munich/London/New York: Prestel.

Green 1998
Green, Nancy [1998]. *Du Sentier à la 7ème avenue. La confection et les immigrés, Paris-New-York, 1880-1980*. Paris: Seuil.

Hakim 1998
Hakim, Catherine [1998]. *Social Change and Innovation in the Labour Market: Evidence from the Census SARS on Occupational Segregation and Labour Mobility, Part-Time Work and Student Jobs, Homework and Self-Employment*. Oxford: Oxford University Press.

Hardyment 1988
Hardyment, Christina [1988]. *From mangle to microwave: the mechanization of household work*, Cambridge & Oxford [UK]: Polity Press. New York: Basil Blackwell.

Hartog 2003
Hartog, François [2003]. *Régimes d'historicité. Présentisme et expérience du temps*. Paris: Seuil.

Holliss 2007
Holliss, Frances [2007]. *The workhome... a new building type?*, PhD thesis, London: London Metropolitan University.

Holliss 2010
Holliss, Frances [2010]. From Longhouse to Live/Work Unit: Parallel Histories and Absent Narratives, *Built from below: British architecture and the vernacular*. Peter Guillery, ed. London/New York: Routledge.

Holliss 2015
Holliss, Frances [2015]. *Beyond Live/Work: The Architecture of Home-Based Work*. London/New York: Routledge.

Holliss 2017
Holliss, Frances [2017]. Designing for Home-Based Work - Lessons from Two English Villages, *Architecture and Culture*, vol. 5, no. 1.

Holliss 2021
Holliss, Frances [2021]. Working from Home, *Built Environment*, vol. 47, no. 3.

Holliss 2022
Holliss, Frances [2022], A House for Artists, *Architecture Today*. 2022. Available at: architecturetoday.co.uk/a-house-for-artists-apparata-barking/. [Accessed 27 April 2023].

Holliss and Barac 2021
Holliss, Frances and Barac, Matthew [2021]. *Housing Space Use in the Pandemic and After: The Case for New Design Guidance*. London: London Metropolitan University. Available at: workhomeproject.org/projects/housing-space-use-in-the-pandemic-and-after-the-case-for-new-design-guidance/. [Accessed 27 April 2023].

Illich 1973
Ivan Illich, Ivan [1973]. *Tools for conviviality*. London: Calder and Boyars.

Illich 1981
Illich, Ivan (1981). *Shadow work*. Boston-London: M. Boyars.

Jarreau 1985
Jarreau, Philippe (1985). *Du bricolage: archéologie de la maison*. Paris: CCI-Centre Pompidou.

Jarrige and Chalmin 2008
Jarrige, François and Chalmin, Cécile (2008). L'émergence du contremaître. L'ambivalence d'une autorité en construction dans l'industrie textile française (1800-1860). *Le Mouvement Social*, vol. III, no. 224, pp. 47-60. Available at: cairn.info/revue-le-mouvement-social-2008-3-page-47.htm#no11. [Accessed 1 May 2023].

Jencks and Silver 2013
Jencks, Charles and Silver, Nathan (2013). *Adhocism: the case for improvisation*. Expanded and updated edition. Cambridge, Massachusetts: MIT Press. [Originally published in 1972].

Kalifa 2013
Kalifa, Dominique (2013). *Les bas-fonds. Histoire d'un imaginaire*. Paris: Seuil.

Knott 2011
Knott, Stephen D. (2011). Amateur Craft as a Differential Practice. PhD thesis under the direction of Hans Stofer at the Royal College of Art and Glenn Adamson at the Victoria & Albert Museum. London.

Koolhaas 2020
Koolhaas, Rem (2020). AMO, *Countryside, A Report*, published on the occasion of the exhibition *Countryside, The Future*, The Solomon R. Guggenheim Museum, New York (20 February - 14 August 2020). Cologne: Taschen.

Kundert 2023
Kundert, Adrianus (2023). *Basketclub*, limited edition. Netherlands: Adrianus Kundert United Enterprises.

Labrusse 2018
Labrusse, Rémi (2018). Des pièces d'époque aux capsules temporelles. Temps historique et temps vécu dans l'expérience esthétique. *Gradhiva*, no. 28, pp. 76-111.

Lacourte 2023
Lacourte, Alexis (2023). For Happy People Only. *Technikart*, 9 February 2023. Available at: pressreader.com/france/technikart/2023 0209/282832195273791 [Accessed 24 April 2023].

Leroi and Mettetal 2023
Leroi, Pascale and Mettetal, Lucile (Eds.) (2023). *À distance. La révolution du télétravail*. Paris: PUF.

Lesme 2014
Lesme, Anne (2014). Lewis Hine et le *National Child Labor Committee:* vérité documentaire et rhétorique visuelle et textuelle. *Transatlantica*, no. 2, published online on 19 February 2015. [Accessed 11 April 2023].

Lorenzetti 2012
Lorenzetti, Luigi (2012). Ruralité, industrie et formes de pluriactivité : une approche comparative. Valais [Switzerland] et Valtellina [Italy], 1860-1930. *Histoire, Économie et Société*, no. 3, pp. 67-83.

LRR 2005
London Residential Research (2005). *Review of Live-Work Policy in Hackney*, London: London Borough of Hackney.

Mendels 1984
Mendels, Franklin (1984). Des industries rurales à la proto-industrie, histoire d'un changement de perspectives. *Annales ESC*, pp. 977-1008.

Midal 2003
Midal, Alexandra (2003). *Antidesign. Petite histoire de la capsule d'habitation en images*. Paris: Épithème.

Midal 2009
Midal, Alexandra (2009). *Design. Introduction à l'histoire d'une discipline* [Design. Introduction to the history of a discipline]. Paris: Pocket.

Mongin 2022
Mongin, Antonin (2022). L'Artisanat d'art du cheveu coupé : Le cheveu comme matière à création d'une recherche par la pratique du design textile [The art of cutting hair: hair as a creative material for research into textile design practice]. PhD thesis, Paris: SACRe-PSL and EnsADLAB.

Montjaret 2000
Montjaret, Anne (2000). Le temps des objets "amicaux", in exh. cat., Paris 2000, pp. 178-180.

Moreno 2020
Moreno, Carlos (2020). *Droit de cité: de la ville-monde à la ville du quart d'heure*. Paris: L'Observatoire.

Munn 1999
Munn, Geoffrey C. (1999). *The Triumph of Love: Jewelry 1530-1930*, London/New York: Thames & Hudson.

OECD 2021
OECD (Organisation for Economic Co-operation and Development) (2021). *Teleworking in the COVID-19 Pandemic: Trends and Prospects*, OECD (oecd.org/coronovirus). Available at: oecd.org/coronavirus/policy-responses/teleworking-in-the-covid-19-pandemic-trends-and-prospects-72a416b6/. [Accessed 27 April 2023].

ONS 2014
Office for National Statistics (2014). *Characteristics of Home Workers*. Available at: webarchive.nationalarchives.gov/uk/ukgwa/20160107085351, ons.gov.uk/ons/rel/lmac/characteristics-of-home-workers/2014/rpt-home-workers.html. [Accessed 27 April 2023].

ONS 2021
Office for National Statistics (2021). *Coronavirus, the UK economy and society, faster indicators: 23 April 2020*. Available at: ons.gov.uk/peoplepopulationandcommunity/healthandsocialcare/conditionsanddiseases/bulletins/coronavirustheukeconomyandsocietyfasterindicator/23april2020 [Accessed 23 April 2020].

Parker and Pascual 2002
Parker, Cheryl and Pascual, Amelita (2002). A voice that could not be ignored: community GIS and gentrification battles in San Francisco. *Community Participation and Geographical Information Systems*. William J. Craig, Trevor M. Harris and Daniel Weiner (Eds.). London: CRC Press.

Perrot 2009
Perrot, Michelle (2009). *Histoire de chambres*. Paris: Seuil.

Pesce 1986
Pesce, Gaetano (1986). Interview with Marie-Jeanne Geyer, *Gaetano Pesce*, 1975-1985, exhibition cat., Marie-Jeanne Geyer (ed.). Musée d'Art moderne, Strasbourg (29 May-17 August 1986), Musée d'Art moderne, Strasbourg, pp. 9-26.

Petiot 2012
Petiot, Fabien (2012). La maîtrise, à bonne distance. Sur la place de la fragilité et de l'imperfection dans le design. Dissertation. Paris: ENSCI-Les Ateliers.

Petiot 2016
Petiot, Fabien (2016). Ergonomie du politique. Quand la forme suit l'exercice des fonctions. Marc Bayard and Brigitte Flamand (Eds.), *Le design du pouvoir. L'Atelier de Recherche et de Création du Mobilier national*, pp. 30-49. Paris: Mare & Marin.

Petiot and Braunstein-Kriegel 2018
Petiot, Fabien and Braunstein-Kriegel, Chloé (Eds.) (2018). *Crafts. Today's Anthology for Tomorrow's Crafts*. Paris: Norma.

Raworth 2017
Raworth, Kate (2017). *Doughnut economics: seven ways to think like a 21st-century economist*. London: Random House Business Books.

Revault 2011
Revault, Myriam (2011). Hannah Arendt penseur de la crise, *Études*, vol. 415, no. 9, pp. 197-206.

Rifkin 2014
Rifkin, Jeremy (2014). *The zero marginal cost society: the internet of things, the collaborative commons, and the eclipse of capitalism*. New York: Palgrave Macmillan.

Roche 1981
Roche, Daniel (1981). *Le peuple de Paris*. Paris: Aubier.

Saunier 1992
Saunier, Pierre-Yves (1992). Lyon au XIXe siècle : les espaces d'une cité. PhD thesis in history, under the directorship of Yves Lequin, pp. 226-228. Lyon: Université Lumière Lyon.

Schneider and Till 2016
Schneider, Tatjana and Till, Jeremy (2016). *Flexible housing*. London: Routledge.

Scholliers and Gubin 1996
Scholliers, Peter and Gubin, Eliane (1996). La crise linière des Flandres. Ouvriers à domicile et prolétariat urbain (1840-1900), *Revue belge de philologie et d'histoire*, vol. 74, no. 2, pp. 365-401.

Schwartz Cowan 1983
Schwartz Cowan, Ruth (1983). *More Work For*

Mother: The Ironies Of Household Technology From The Open Hearth To The Microwave. New York: Basic Books.

Serfaty-Garzon 2005
Serfaty-Garzon, Perla (2005). *Chez-soi, les territoires de l'intimité*. Paris: Armand Colin.

Syvil 2020
SYVIL [Architecture and urban planning studio) (2020). *Faire place à de nouvelles architectures du stock et de la production*. In exh. cat. Paris 2020 p. 33.

Steer 1950
Steer, Francis W. (1950). *Farm and cottage inventories of mid-Essex*, 1635-1749. Chelmsford: Essex County Council.

Terrier 1996
Terrier, Didier (1996). *Les deux âges de la proto-industrie. Les tisserands du Cambrésis et du Saint-Quentinois*, 1730-1880. Paris: EHESS.

Terrier 1998
Terrier, Didier (1998). La dispersion rurale du travail textile en France : logique d'implantation et gestion d'un espace productif, 1650-1780. In Vincenzo Giura [Ed.], *Gli insediamenti Economici e le Loro Logiche*. Naples: Edizioni Scientifiche Italiane, pp. 97-106.

Terrier 2021
Terrier Didier (2021). Villageois occupés d'industrie en Europe occidentale (1830-1930): des ouvriers hors champ? *La casquette et le marteau. Nouveaux regards sur le travail en Europe occidentale* (1830-1930). Paris: Bréal pp. 13-34.

Terrier and Maitte 2020
Terrier, Didier and Maitte, Corine (2020). *Les rythmes du labeur - Enquête sur le temps de travail en Europe occidentale, XIVe - XIXe siècles*. Paris: La Dispute.

Thiesse 1995
Thiesse, Anne-Marie (1995). Organisation des loisirs des travailleurs et temps dérobés (1880-1930). Alain Corbin (ed.), *L'avènement des loisirs. 1850-1960*. Paris: Aubier. pp. 302-322.

Thomas 2022
Jules Thomas, Entre télétravail et "flex office", Deloitte abandonne un nouvel immeuble à la City de Londres. *Le Monde*, 20 April 2022, p. 20.

Toffler 1972
Toffler, Alvin (1972), *Future shock*. London: Pan Books (Originally published in 1970)

Toffler 1980
Toffler, Alvin (1980). *The Third Wave*. New York: William Morrow.

TUC 2021
TUC (2021). *The Future of Flexible Work*. London: Trades Union Council.

VeloCity (A)
VeloCity (2019). *Growing Villages Differently - manifesto for the 21st Century Village*. Available at: velocity651476576.files.wordpress.com/2020/03/veocity_modern-day-picturesque_final.pdf.

VeloCity (B)
Modern Day Picturesque: VeloCity (2020). *Existing and emerging models of rural densification*. Available at: velocity651476576.files.wordpress.com/2020/05/velocity_manifesto_may2020.pdf.

Vernant 2004
Vernant, Jean-Pierre (2004). *La traversée des frontières*. Paris: Le Seuil.

VOXEU CEPR 2021
VOXEU CEPR [Centre for Economic Policy Research] (2021). *Working from home during the COVID-19 pandemic: Updating global estimates using household survey data*. Sergi Soares, Florence Bonnet and Janine Berg [Eds.]. Available at: voxeu.org/ article/working-home-during-covid-19-pandemic-updated-estimates. [Accessed 25 April 2021].

Woolf 2020
Virginia Woolf, Virginia (2020). *A Room of One's Own*. London: Renard Press Ltd [Originally published in 1929].

Zukin 1988
Zukin, Sharon (1988). *Loft Living: Culture and Capital in Urban Change*. London: Radius.

EXHIBITION CATALOGUES

New York 1972
Ambasz, Emilio, ed. (1972) *Italy: The New Domestic Landscape. Achievements and Problems of Italian Design*. New York: MoMa. Published following the exhibition *Italy: The New*

Domestic Landscape at MoMa, New York (26 May-11 September 1972).

Paris 2000
Guidot, Raymond and Jousset, Marie-Laure, eds. (2000). *Les bons génies de la vie domestique*. Published following the exhibition *Les bons génies de la vie domestique* at the Centre Pompidou in Paris (11 October 2000-22 January 2001).

Paris 2014
Encore Heureux, ed. (2014). *Matière grise : matériaux, réemploi, architecture*. Published following the exhibition *Matière grise : matériaux, réemploi, architecture* at the Pavillon de l'Arsenal, Paris (26 September 2014-25 January 2015).

Paris 2016
Leloup, Jean-Yves, ed. (2016). *Electrosound: machines, musiques & culture(s)*. Marseille/Paris: Le Mot et le reste/Fondation groupe EDF. Published following the Electrosound: machines, musiques & culture(s) exhibition at the Espace Fondation EDF (25 May - 2 October 2016).

Paris 2018
SOA/Rosenstiehl, Augustin, eds. (2018). *Capital agricole. Chantiers pour une ville cultivée*. Paris: Pavillon de l'Arsenal. Published following the *Capital agricole. Chantiers pour une ville cultivée* exhibition held at the Pavillon de l'Arsenal, Paris (2 October 2018 - 17 February 2019).

Paris 2019
Houzé, Guillaume and Quintin, François, eds. (2019). *Hella Jongerius. Interlacing. Une recherche tissée / Interlace. Woven Research*. Paris: Lafayette Anticipations, Fondation d'entreprise Galeries Lafayette; London: Koenig Books. Published following the exhibition *Hella Jongerius. Interlacing. Une recherche tissée / Interlace. Woven Research* at Lafayette Anticipations in Paris (7 June - 8 September 2019).

Paris 2020
Et demain, on fait quoi ? 198 propositions pour penser la ville (2020). Paris: Pavillon de l'Arsenal. Published following the exhibition *Et demain, on fait quoi ? 198 propositions pour penser la ville* held at the Pavillon de l'Arsenal in Paris (18 April - 19 June 2020).

Paris 2023
Musée des Arts Décoratifs (MAD) and Bruna, Denis, eds. (2023). *Des cheveux et des poils*. Paris: MAD. Published following the exhibition *Des cheveux et des poils* held at the MAD in Paris (5 April - 17 September 2023).

Rouen 2020
Bosc, Alexandra, ed. (2020). La céramique pour toutes. Femmes et pratiques artisanales amateur dans la seconde moitié Du XIXe siècle. In *Camille Moreau-Nélaton. Une femme céramiste au temps des impressionnistes*. Milan: Silvana Editoriale, pp. 29-40. Published following the exhibition *Camille Moreau-Nélaton. Une femme céramiste au temps des impressionnistes* held at the Musée de la céramique in Rouen (3 April - 7 September 2020).

Strasbourg 1986
Geyer, Marie-Jeanne, ed. (1986). *Gaetano Pesce, 1975-1985*, Strasbourg: Musée d'Art moderne. Published following the exhibition *Gaetano Pesce, 1975-1985* at the Musée d'Art moderne in Strasbourg (29 May - 17 August 1986).

AUDIOVISUAL SOURCES

Dominici 2021
Dominici, Michèle, director, (2021). *L'Histoire oubliée des femmes au foyer*. Documentary, 52 mins. From ARTE France and Squawk.

Thomas 2006
Thomas, Jérôme, director, (2006). *Home studio: the musical revolution*. Documentary, 72 min. From Folistar (Paris) (2006).

Dannoritzer 2010
Dannoritzer, Cosima, director (2010), *Prêt à jeter (Kaufen für die Müllhalde)*. Documentary, 75 mins. From ARTE France, Radio Televisión Espanola and Televisió de Catalunya (2010).

CREDITS

Cover: © Emma Cogné / © Benoît Jacquemin

Fig. 1 : © Martial Marquet (design) / © Mario Simon Lafleur (photo)

Fig. 2 : © Courtesy Marie Jacotey and Hannah Barry Gallery, London

Fig. 3 : © Wald

Fig. 4 : © gallica.bnf.fr / Bibliothèque nationale de France

Fig. 5 : © Photo Gouttefangeas. Tous droits réservés / Éditions G d'O. Archives départementales du Puy-de-Dôme, fonds Gouttefangeas, 569 Fi 1061

Fig. 6, 7, 8, 9, 10 : © Collection Mundaneum, Mons

Fig. 11, 12, 13 : © Frances Holliss

Fig. 14, 15 : © Stole Eriksen

Fig. 16 : © Industriemuseum, Gent

Fig. 17, 18 : © RMN-Grand Palais (Limoges, musée national Adrien Dubouché) / Mathieu Rabeau

Fig. 19 : © Universiteitsbibliotheek Gent BIB. AFF.C.000076

Fig. 20 : © Collection Mundaneum, Mons

Fig. 21 : © Bold

Fig. 22 : © Industriemuseum, Gent

Fig. 23 : © Archives INA (Institut national de l'audiovisuel), France

Fig. 24 : © Industriemuseum, Gent

Fig. 25 : © Mucem / Daniel Frasnay

Fig. 26 : © Musée d'histoire de Lyon – Gadagne

Fig. 27 : © Cité internationale de la Tapisserie et de l'Art tissé, Aubusson, France / Institut Français de la Mode / Made in Town

Fig. 28 : © Mucem / Denise Sussfeld

Fig. 29 : © Laura Fiorio

Fig. 30 : © Studio Brieditis & Evans

Fig. 31 : © Iris Seuren

Fig. 32 : © Industriemuseum, Gent

Fig. 33 : © Atelier Baudelaire

Fig. 34 : © Centraal Museum Utrecht / © Djoke de Jong & Droog Design

Fig. 35 : © Stephane Bureaux (design) / © Thomas Duval (photo)

Fig. 36 : Collection CID au Grand-Hornu

Fig. 37 : © Rod Hünt, Ivan Nascimento, Ric Allen and The Restart Project

Fig. 38 : © Luc Deriez / Repair Together

Fig. 39, 40 : © Christopher Woodcock

Fig. 41, 42 : © Antonin Mongin

Fig. 43, 44 : © Jean-Claude Planchet

Fig. 45 : Collection CID au Grand-Hornu

Fig. 46, 47 : © Lotte Dekker & Gieke van Lon / Humade

Fig. 48 : © Stephane Bureaux (design) / © Thomas Duval (photo)

Fig. 49 : Collection CID au Grand-Hornu

Fig. 50 : © Studio Bouroullec / Philippe Thibault

Fig. 51 : © Will & Tom Butterfield

Fig.52 : © Benjamin Edgar / Will & Tom Butterfield

Fig. 53 : © Studio Michael Schoner

Fig. 54 : © Sylvain Willenz

Fig. 55, 56 : © Erwan Bouroullec

Fig. 57 : © Christian van der Kooy

Fig. 58 : © Hella Jongerius / Jongeriuslab

Fig. 59 : © Studio BrichetZiegler

Fig. 60 : © Rive Roshan

Fig. 61 : © Shigeki Fujishiro

Fig. 62 : © Carole Baijings

Fig. 63 : © Studio Simone Post

Fig. 64 : © Rein Reitsma

Fig. 65 : © Studio Bertjan Pot

Fig. 66 : © Adrianus Kundert

Fig. 67 : © Studio Chris Kabel

Fig. 68 : © Wald

Fig. 69 : © The Heath Robinson Museum

Fig. 70 : © The Museum of Modern Art, New York/Scala, Florence

Fig. 71, 72 : © Wald

Fig. 73, 74 : © Marco Federico Cagnoni

Fig. 75, 76 : © Ciguë

Fig. 77, 78 : © Emma Cogné

Fig. 79 : © Studio Makkink & Bey (design) / © Kristof Vrancken (photo)

Fig. 80 : © The Heath Robinson Museum

Fig. 81 : © Assemble

Fig. 82 : © Courtesy Marie Jacotey and Hannah Barry Gallery, London

Fig. 83 : © VeloCity

Fig. 84 : © David Leon Fiene

Fig. 85 : © Studio Makkink & Bey

Fig. 86 : © VeloCity

ACKNOWLEDGEMENTS

LENDERS

Creators and institutions have contributed to this exhibition through warm and stimulating discussions. From a scientific point of view to logistical support, they have been our companions throughout this project. We would like to express our gratitude to them for what were, above all, precious encounters. They include:

Institutions

BELGIUM
— Industrie Museum, Ghent
— Universiteits Bibliotheek, Ghent
— Mundaneum, Mons

FRANCE
— Cité de la tapisserie, Aubusson
— Musée national Adrien Dubouché, Limoges - Cité de la céramique, Sèvres and Limoges
— Gadagne - Lyon History Museum
— MUCEM, Marseille
— Musée Electropolis, Mulhouse
— Cinémathèque, Paris
— MNAM-Centre Georges Pompidou, Paris
— INA, Paris
— Françoise Jollant Kneebone, Paris

GERMANY
— Gropius Bau, Berlin

GREAT BRITAIN
— Heath Robinson Museum, Pinner
— Studio Aardman, Bristol
— Cultureshock, London

NETHERLANDS
— TextielMuseum, Tilburg
— Centraal Museum, Utrecht

SWITZERLAND
— Gewerbemuseum, Winterthur

UNITED STATES
— Disney Pictures

Designers and privates

— Assemble (Owen Lacey, Mary Anderson, Naomi Crédé)
— Marta Ayala Herrera
— Carole Baijings
— Camille Baudelaire
— Bold Design
— Erwan Bouroullec
— Stéphane Bureaux
— Tom et Will Butterfield
— Studio BrichetZiegler
— Marco Federico Cagnoni
— Ciguë (Camille Besse, Alphonse Sarthout et Camille Bénard)
— Emma Cogné
— Studio Evans & Brieditis (Katharina Evans and Katharina Brieditis)
— Luc Deriez
— Shigeki Fuijshiro
— Mateo Fumero
— Humade (Lotte Dekker)
— Marie Jacotey
— Studio Hella Jongerius, assisted by Amanda Fitz-James
— Chris Kabel
— Adrianus Kundert

- Studio Makkink & Bey (Jürgen Bey and Rianne Makkink)
- Martial Marquet Studio
- Omayra Maymo
- Isaac Pineiro Meira
- Antonin Mongin
- Simone Post
- Rein Reitsma
- Rive Roshan (Ruben de la Rive Box, Golnar Roshan and Ava)
- Michael Schoner
- Iris Seuren
- Jérôme Thomas
- Emmanuel van der Bruggen
- Christian van der Kooy
- Velocity (Petra Marko and Sarah Featherstone Young)
- Sanna Völker
- Wald City (Frédérique Barchelard and Flavien Menu)
- Sylvain Willenz

AUTHORS' ACKNOWLEDGEMENTS

From idea to reality, we were able to count on the enthusiasm and energy of the teams at the CID-Grand Hornu, and the attentiveness and creativity of set designers Sam Baron and Sophie Albert.

Our warmest thanks to them.

Others lent their time and knowledge, not their works. We are very grateful to the specialists who agreed to contribute to this exhibition and its catalogue. First and foremost Arianne Aujoulat, Frances Holliss, Antonin Mongin, Didier Terrier and Christophe Vix-Gras for their texts and the difficult task of synthesising the vast subjects that occupy them; thanks also to Jean-Charles Hameau, Michel Lagarde, Jean-Yves Leloup and Marie-Pauline Martin, and Jean-Claude Planchet, true 'facilitators' whose advice enabled us to make discoveries and encounters. Finally, we are indebted to our friends, spouses and parents for their affection and encouragement, as well as their assiduous proofreading: Alexandra Bosc, Adrianne Cairns, Françoise Jollant Kneebone, Emmanuel Kriegel and Alma Etty Kriegel.

Thank you all so much!

Editorial concept & coordination
Fabien Petiot and Chloé Braunstein-Kriegel

Authors
Fabien Petiot and Chloé Braunstein-Kriegel
Frances Holliss
Antonin Mongin
Didier Terrier
Christophe Vix-Gras

Translation
Alpito
Right-Ink

Graphic design
Pink Monstera – Laetitia Centritto
Catarina Carreiras (logotype)

Editing
CID at Grand-Hornu
Alexandra Bosc
Françoise Jollant Kneebone
Adrianne Cairns

This book was published as part of the exhibition *Home Made - Create, Produce, Live* curated by Fabien Petiot and Chloé Braunstein-Kriegel; presented by the CID - centre for innovation and design at Grand-Hornu (Belgium)
from 15 October 2023 to 11 February 2024

Curators
Fabien Petiot and Chloé Braunstein-Kriegel

Scenography
Sam Baron and Sophie Albert

Production
The non-profit association CID - centre for innovation and design at Grand-Hornu is subsidised by the Province of Hainaut.
With the support of the Wallonia-Brussels Federation, Visual Arts Sector.

Published
CID - centre for innovation and design at Grand-Hornu
Rue Sainte-Louise 82
B-7301 Hornu, Belgique
www.cid-grand-hornu.be
Facebook - Instagram : cidgrandhornu

Stichting Kunstboek bv
Legeweg 165
B-8020 Oostkamp
www.stichtingkunstboek.com

Printed in the EU

Any reproduction or adaptation of any part of this book by printing, photocopying, microfilming or any other process without the written permission of the publisher is strictly illegal.

ISBN : 978-90-5856-712-3
NUR : 656
D/2023/6407/18